Further Praise for
Whole-Child Teaching: A Framework for Meeting the Needs of Today's Students

"James Trifone clearly presents what most educators in the trenches, so to speak, would agree should be the future of education in this country. He is clear on what needs to be done moving forward. Most administrators encourage their teachers top teach 21st century but don't give them the tools to do so. This is the text Administrators should be exploring with their staff as a guidebook to teaching 21st century skills."

—**Ingrid Baron**, special education educator

"This is the book I have been waiting for someone to write and I am sure many educators would agree. As a teacher who has been in this profession for 27 years and witnessed first-hand the damage and turmoil that has ensued over the two and a half decades, the book validated so many of my beliefs and hopes for change. I am always so grateful that we have people like Jim who continue to speak up and fight for what is best for our children."

—**Melissa Costantini**, kindergarten educator

Whole-Child Teaching

Whole-Child Teaching

A Framework for Meeting the Needs of Today's Students

James D. Trifone

ROWMAN & LITTLEFIELD
Lanham • Boulder • New York • London

Published by Rowman & Littlefield
An imprint of The Rowman & Littlefield Publishing Group, Inc.
4501 Forbes Boulevard, Suite 200, Lanham, Maryland 20706
www.rowman.com

6 Tinworth Street, London SE11 5AL, United Kingdom

Copyright © 2021 by James D. Trifone

All rights reserved. No part of this book may be reproduced in any form or by any electronic or mechanical means, including information storage and retrieval systems, without written permission from the publisher, except by a reviewer who may quote passages in a review.

British Library Cataloguing in Publication Information Available

Library of Congress Cataloging-in-Publication Data

Names: Trifone, James D., 1952– author.
Title: Whole-child teaching : a framework for meeting the needs of today's students / James D. Trifone.
Description: Lanham : Rowman & Littlefield, [2021] | Includes bibliographical references and index. | Summary: "This book provides an in-depth discussion of the aspects of a whole-child learner paradigm including how educator and school-based influences interrelate with personal and interpersonal demonstrations of learning to create a holistic learning system."—Provided by publisher.
Identifiers: LCCN 2021000791 (print) | LCCN 2021000792 (ebook) | ISBN 9781475861167 (cloth) | ISBN 9781475861174 (paperback) | ISBN 9781475861181 (epub)
Subjects: LCSH: Holistic education. | Student-centered learning. | Interdisciplinary approach in education. | Learning, Psychology of.
Classification: LCC LC990.T77 2021 (print) | LCC LC990 (ebook) | DDC 370.11—dc23
LC record available at https://lccn.loc.gov/2021000791
LC ebook record available at https://lccn.loc.gov/2021000792

Contents

Foreword	xi
Preface	xv
Acknowledgments	xix
Introduction	1
I: Whether to Reform or Transform, That Is the Question	**5**
1 America Needs to *Transform* Rather Than *Reform* Education	7
What's Wrong with American Education?	7
Test, Test, Test: The Flaw in the Vision	11
Who's to Blame for the Underachievement of American Students?	12
The Emergence of a Culture of Learning and Thinking	13
Today's Students Need Different Skills to Thrive in the Twenty-First Century	14
Summary	16
2 Transformation Requires a Systemic Change	19
Nature of Systems in Response to Change	19
Educational Systems Are "Living Processes"	21
Changing the System Means Aligning All Components	21
What Is Needed Today Is a Systemic Transformation in Education	22
The Role of Disruption in Systemic Change	23
Computer-Based Learning (CBL) as a Disruptive Force in Education	24
Project-Based Learning as a Disruptive Force in Education	26
Place-Based Education (PBE) as a Disruptive Force in Education	27
Summary	32

3 Transforming Education: The Whole-Child Paradigm 33
  What's a Paradigm? 33
  Education Is in a Muddle 34
  The Learning Compact Renewed: Whole Child for the Whole World 35
  The Whole-Child Learner Paradigm 37
  Summary 42

II: The District-Based Influences That Affect Learning and Thinking 43

4 Creating a New Story of Learning and Thinking 45
  Learning as Product or Process? 45
  A Whole-Child Educational Framework 46
  An Authentic Curriculum 47
  Why Do We Educate in the First Place? 48
  What Does a "Quality" Education Mean? 50
  What Are the Metaphors of the Twentieth-Century Educational Story? 51
  Orientations on Classroom Thinking and Learning 51
  What Is the Twentieth-Century-Story Being "Told" in Most American Classrooms? 52
  What Is the Twenty-first-Century Story We Want to "Tell" in American Classrooms? 53
  Summary 54

III: The Educator-Based Influences That Affect Learning and Thinking 57

5 What Are the Teaching Practices of the Teacher-Centered and Learner-Centered Approaches to Teaching? 59
  Twentieth-Century Classroom Teaching Practices: Learning as Product 59
  Twenty-first-Century Classroom Teaching Practices: Learning as Process 62
  Summary 65

6 Toward a Constructivist Approach to Learning 67
  Whole-Child Education and Constructivism 67
  Guided Improvisation 70
  Summary 71

7 What Thinking Skills Foster Meaningful Learning 73
  Teacher-Centered versus Whole-Child Learning 73
  Encouraging Meaningful Learning and Thinking 74
  What Are the Learning and Thinking Skills Needed to Thrive in the Twenty-first Century? 76

Twenty-First-Century Exemplar Schools	85
Summary	86
8 The Interdisciplinary Curriculum	**89**
Truth, Beauty, and Goodness	89
The Arts: A Bridge to Interdisciplinary Learning	90
Summary	93
9 Why Is the Learner-Centered Educator Interested in Positive Education?	**95**
What Is Positive Psychology?	95
Positive Education	96
How Can the Learner-Centered Educator Foster Competency in Social and Emotional Learning (SEL) Skills?	100
Developing Competency in Social and Emotional Skills	100
School-Based Brief Positive Psychological Interventions (BPPIs)	101
Summary	106

IV: Personal Demonstrations of Learning and Thinking	**107**
10 The Whole-Child Educator Fosters a Growth Mindset	**109**
What Does It Take to Motivate Learners?	109
Growth Versus Fixed Mindsets	110
Summary	114

V: Interpersonal Demonstrations of Learning and Thinking	**115**
11 How Do Students Demonstrate Competency in Interpersonal Skills?	**117**
The Coddling of American Students	118
Character Strengths	121
What Is Emotional Intelligence?	122
Summary	125

Afterword	127
References	129
Index	141
About the Author	149

Foreword

Jim's book, *Whole-Child Teaching*, presents an in-depth, comprehensive review of the major initiatives he experienced as a public high school teacher of forty-two years, years that spanned the twentieth and twenty-first centuries. I have experienced them, too, in roughly the same fifty-year period, from the early 1970s until now, first as a teacher and then as a teacher-trainer, administrator, and state-level policy leader.

Why did I agree to read Jim's book carefully and write this foreword? I wanted to see if and how our perspectives dovetailed and how those perspectives might affect a vision of education in the United States.

Jim shows us that some of the initiatives seemed disparate; some seemed counter to each other. But at their core many of them were connected—and Jim found those connections. He exhorts us to abandon those not supportive of whole-child initiatives and maintain and strengthen the connectedness of those that do. This, he argues, will require a paradigm shift.

Jim's basic premise is that schools have to change fundamentally. He argues that schools must be "transformed," not "merely reformed," in a systemic way in order to move from a twentieth-century, teacher-centered environment to a twenty-first-century, student-centered environment that addresses the needs of the "whole child." He maintains that only in that way will we return to being global leaders in education, a distinction he shows the United States has lost. I agree.

Interestingly, what he argues has been done successfully in Finland, a country whose schools I have visited three times with teacher leaders from Connecticut and North Carolina because it is viewed as one of the global leaders in education. Pasi Sahlberg is the author of *Finnish Lessons 2.0*. In his foreword to Tim Walker's book, *Teach Like Finland*, he describes what accounts for the great success of Finland's schools. Sahlberg writes, "First, we argue that the comprehensive school that children start when they turn seven provides balanced, holistic, and child-focused education and development to all children. . . . The curriculum in Finnish schools addresses all subjects evenly and thereby provides all children with opportunities to cultivate multiple aspects of their personalities and talents."

In other words, at the core, Finnish education embraces what Jim describes as essential for the United States.

As he takes us through a detailed explanation of the many programs (such as project-based learning) that incorporate elements of the whole-child doctrine, Jim draws the distinction that in teaching it is process rather than product that matters. Further, he presents "the Whole-Child Learner Paradigm" in which all the elements are interdependent. Teachers who foster social and emotional skills as well as a growth mindset, for example, would not be doing this on their own but would be "supported and championed by the entire educational system."

Why did I decide to write the foreword to this book?

First, I believe in its basic premise, that children learn best when actively involved with others in pursuing their interests and passions in ways that allow them to explore and figure out many possible solutions to important problems (a.k.a. the "whole-child" approach).

Second, I believe that *right now*, before we go back to school after COVID, is the opportune time for communities to pivot and envision *what education should be*.

Third, *right now*, after we have lived through an unprecedented time of political, racial, and emotional strife and upheaval, is the time to ask ourselves what underlying causes—including how we have educated our citizenry—created the conditions in which such behavior flourished and how we can address them.

Jim's book will have been a success if his analysis of education in the past fifty years or so—and his proposition about what we should pivot to and how we should do that—spurs all of us to think comprehensively and act to transform our education system with these questions in mind:

- What is essential for kids to know and do?
- How do kids pursue their passions and interests and contribute positively to society?
- What is essential to create an informed, caring citizenry?
- How do kids have fun, take risks, and persevere while learning?
- How do kids show kindness, caring, compassion, respect, integrity, and honesty to themselves and others?

Our "classrooms," our "schools," are different now in the age of COVID. Our relationships, our interactions, and our communications are different now in the age of COVID. When we "go back," it must be to something different and better for us all.

If Jim's analysis and vision help us envision what education should be for children in our communities, then Jim has done his job.

Dr. Betty J. Sternberg
Connecticut Commissioner of Education, Emerita
Director, Teacher Leader Fellowship Program,
Central Connecticut State University

Preface

This book offers an alternative story to the adequate but nonetheless teacher-centered, "one size fits all" storyline that held sway over educators throughout the twentieth century. The central feature of this narrative rests on demanding a systemic change to how we teach students in the twenty-first century. Lying at the heart of this new narrative is what I hope will be perceived as a persuasive rationale for ushering in a paradigm shift in education. America is no longer considered to be the global educational vanguard. Rather, we have succumbed to the notion that knowledge is a commodity and, as such, can be packaged and delivered to students. Therefore, standardized testing and adopting a "one size fits all" educational approach have come to be the norm.

The motivation for writing this book emerged over a period of several years. As a veteran high school teacher, I became disillusioned with the reform initiatives of No Child Left Behind (NCLB) and Race to the Top (RTTT). The latter stipulated that state grant money would only be issued by adopting and committing to implement systemic education reform. The problem was that "systemic reform" remained limited to only what could be assessed on standardized tests.

The most recent national education reform effort emerged in 2015 with the Obama administration's Every Student Succeeds Act (ESSA). ESSA offered more state control over assessing learning. It also offered opportunities to equitably provide learning opportunities for all students. These learning opportunities attempted to close the achievement gap. This was particularly the case with students in low-performing school districts. While ESSA was certainly a step in the right direction, it only provided a *partial*, rather than *systemic*, restructuring to support teachers and student learning.

ESSA is certainly a quantum leap forward from the oppressive NCLB, but it still upholds that student achievement is assessed, albeit by fewer standardized tests. Literature studies have concluded that standardized tests have had little to no impact in enhancing the learning. Furthermore, "high-stakes" tests have proven themselves incapable of assessing the essential noncognitive skills. These skills are essential for students to be successful learners and workers in the twenty-first century.

Education reformers speculate that the latest reform initiative "might" better prepare our students to be "college and career" ready. However, what has been assessed on standardized tests is *not* what educators define as "college and career" readiness for the twenty-first century. Familiarity with the works of Howard Gardner, Tony Wagner, or Ken Robinson would have led them to appreciate student needs fundamental to flourish in the twenty-first century. These learning experts have determined the skill sets required to be successful in the twenty-first-century classroom. Moreover, none of these *can* be measured by a standardized test.

In hindsight, classroom educators should have been directly involved in the creation of these reform initiatives. Classroom educators would have contended that many of the skills and competencies required to be effective learners and citizens are not exclusively academic. Rather, noncognitive skills, habits of mind, and learning dispositions, like developing a positive attitude toward learning, need to occur first. This attitude fosters using the imagination and creativity to explore the natural world.

Children are naturally curious and love to learn. Children need to be provided with opportunities that build upon their natural learning tendencies in a positive context. Moreover, these opportunities will better prepare them to understand what they learn.

The current education reform initiative still mandates that children start learning abstract and academic content in kindergarten. Whatever happened to learning how to socialize and resolve conflicts? These were notions Robert Fulghum shared in his classic book *All I Really Need to Know I Learned in Kindergarten*. Education needs to be about developing the *mind, body, and disposition* of learners. If schooling omits any of these, students miss opportunities to grow and mature into successful and happy adults.

Therefore, what needs to be considered as "Common Core" is something very different than what has been promoted. I concluded that a philosophical change was necessary to prepare students for career and college readiness. Toward this end, it is imperative for American educational leaders to embrace a more personalized learning philosophy. What has come to be referred to as the "Common Core" is far too limited in its scope and relevance for today's generation of learners. While some aspects of these standards have merit, others were found to be inappropriate for many, if not most, students.

Fortunately, parents are now recognizing the inadequacies and flawed assumptions of the reform initiatives. They are finally standing up and speaking out to their legislators to demand a course correction for the misdirected national education policy. Colleges are now appreciating that SATs have little predictive value for success in college. Moreover, even the College Board acknowledged that grade point averages are far more predictive of future academic success than the SAT.

Therefore, this book represents my Whole-Child Learner framework for transforming American education. In addition to providing twenty-first-century academic skills, it also addresses the social and emotional skills needed to better cope with a changing world. Toward this end, what is needed is to undertake a systemic change in American education. I hope this book creates a coherent and persuasive argument for this course change in education.

This framework mandates changing a system that promotes mediocrity to one that embraces excellence. Thus this book represents my rationale for embracing a new narrative for education. I hope that in the next few years, we will see a major shift away from a reliance on standardized testing. Moreover, a vital component to a systemic change involves nurturing the development of competent learners, good citizens, and capable workers.

Acknowledgments

This book is the culmination of forty-three years of experience as a public school educator. The world has changed dramatically since I began teaching in the mid-1970s. Over that time, I have been fortunate to have had several mentors who guided and supported me in my career. Therefore, this book could not have been written without the scholarship and insights of many colleagues and authors whose books raised my awareness of the need to propose a systemic change in American education. I owe a debt of gratitude to my esteemed colleagues Peter Concilio, Ingrid Baron, Rebecca Camperlengo, Melissa Costantini, Lorraine Nusdeu, and Dr. Mary Gadd. Their constructive criticism, candor, and reflections contributed to refining my manuscript. Moreover, I want to thank Dr. Betty Sternberg, who took time out of her busy schedule to write the foreword.

I also want to thank Julie Barker, Anne Wellspeak, and Lisa Huber for taking time out of their busy lives to read and endorse my manuscript.

Most of all I want to thank my wife, who has always stood by me over the past thirty-two years. In addition to serving as a loving and compassionate wife and mother to our two daughters (and myriad animals), she has been my counsel, soul mate, friend, and teacher. Thankfully, she has patiently endured three decades living with a scholar whose predilection is to philosophize on just about everything. Lastly, I want to thank my parents for raising me with a strong set of core values, a strong work ethic, optimism, and a love of learning.

Introduction

This book is an orientation for the learner-centered educator seeking to understand how best to teach and foster the development of the whole child. Teaching the whole child means nurturing the development of learners' cognitive, as well as social and emotional, needs. Therefore, the book is organized into five parts each framed by a specific question that addresses either the cognitive, emotional, or social needs of the whole child.

Part I is entitled "Whether to Reform or Transform, That Is the Question." It is framed by the question: "How Did American Education Get Stuck, and How Do We Find Our Way Out of the Quagmire We Are In?" Chapter 1 examines the problems that arise by saddling our schools with an outdated educational philosophy. The structure of our current education system has its origins in the wake of the nineteenth-century Industrial Revolution.

This design worked well preparing children for a future working in factories to mass-produce goods. However, education came to be viewed as a "machine" whereby students could be "processed" and what they learned transformed into "commodities." Lost in this process was the unquantifiable motivational, social, and emotional processes responsible for learning in the first place. The nineteenth-century "clockwork" metaphor became the mechanism for education. This metaphor outlined not only what *would* be taught but also what *could* be taught. Since then education reform movements have been fragmentary, myopic, and still reflective of nineteenth-century thinking.

This book recommends transforming rather than merely reforming American education. In chapter 2, I argue that it is only through a *systemic change* that any major and lasting impact can be made in the effectiveness of American education. Therefore, what is needed is a new educational culture to shift the way we educate. The systemic change would include more learner-centered practices and strategies to personalize learning.

Therefore, the benefits of innovative ways of learning (e.g., computer-based-learning, project-based learning, and place-based education) will be discussed. In order to make a systemic change in American education, a new framework is needed. This Whole-Child framework is offered to displace the current model and redefine *how, why, and what* we teach. Therefore, in chapter 3, the reader will be introduced to the Whole-Child Learner Paradigm. This model distinguishes the learner as situated in social and individual spheres of influence.

Learning is a process that emerges from external factors like educators' pedagogies, curricula, and lesson plans and school structure, vision, and mission. Learning is demonstrated in both personal and interpersonal ways. It is important for the Whole-Child educator to promote a meaningful approach to learning. A meaningful approach fosters the imagination, creativity, and innovative thinking, as well as competency using higher-order thinking skills. Additionally, the Whole-Child educator needs to infuse the development of social and emotional skills, empathy, compassion, and positive education.

The remaining sections are based on sharing the literature findings supporting the Whole-Child Learner Paradigm introduced in part I. Part II is titled "The District-Based Influences That Affect Learning and Thinking." It offers the reader a new story emerging from the Whole-Child Learner paradigm introduced in part I. An innovative educational story requires a new language and therefore metaphors to create a new context. Therefore, this section is framed by the question: "What Are the Metaphors and Values for the Twenty-First-Century Whole-Child Education Story?"

The teacher-centered story views learning as a "product" (noun-based and therefore static). On the other hand, the learning metaphor for the Whole-Child story is learning as a "process" (verb-based and therefore dynamic). Chapter 4 proposes a new story of education. This new narrative emerging from the Whole-Child paradigm is holistic rather than atomistic, interdisciplinary instead of disciplinary, interconnected instead of fragmented. This narrative addresses and develops the social, emotional, as well as cognitive aspects of learners. It requires a discussion of why we educate and what constitutes a "quality" education.

Part III is titled "The Educator-Based Influences That Affect Learning and Thinking." American education is still largely based upon a teacher-centered classroom. Here the teacher is the "sage on the stage" and primarily lectures to "cover" the curriculum. Textbooks serve as the source of what is taught. Students typically work independently on worksheets or activities based on the textbook content. Students take teacher-developed exams, which are intended to assess what students have learned.

The new twenty-first-century digital age Whole-Child story offered here is based on a learner-centered classroom. The Whole-Child teacher embraces a learner-centered approach. In this capacity, the teacher is the "guide on the side" and serves in the role of mentor or coach to aid students. Students work in collaborative groups on interdisciplinary projects. Therefore, the question posed in the five chapters of this section is "How Can a Whole-Child Approach to Teaching Foster Development of the Skills Requisite to Thrive in the Twenty-First Century?"

Chapter 5 examines the teaching practices of the teacher-centered and learner-centered educator. Chapter 6 discusses the educational advantages of constructivist versus instructionist approaches to teaching. In stark contrast to an instructionist teacher-centered approach to learning and thinking, constructivist methods offer a Whole-Child meaningful approach to learning. A constructivist approach promotes imagination, creativity, and innovation along with higher-order thinking skills. Constructivist approaches motivate and engage the learner with relevant and problem-based learning opportunities.

Chapter 7 discusses the skills today's learners will need to imagine, create, innovate, and flourish in the twenty-first century. Chapter 8 presents the significance of an interdisciplinary curriculum. I argue that the arts are the means to integrate all other academic disciplines into a more holistic framework for learning.

While the first three chapters of this section focus on the cognitive factors entailed in the learning process, chapter 9 discusses the emerging science of Positive Psychology and why it offers Whole-Child educators insight into better understanding how best to enhance the well-being of their students. Martin Seligman's PERMA model provides a backdrop for how individuals attain and sustain a sense of well-being. Positive Education, as an outgrowth of Positive Psychology, emphasizes ways to help students flourish, succeed, and realize their full potential. Toward this end, we will explore a unique set of positive character traits that positively impact students' mental health and academic performance.

Part IV is titled "Personal Demonstrations of Learning and Thinking." This part and chapter 10 are framed by the question: "How Can the Whole-Child Educator Motivate Students to Take a Meaningful Approach to Learning?" Why do some learners adopt a rote approach to learning while others adopt a meaningful approach to learning? Is it due to their cognitive ability and/or motivation? These questions lead the Whole-Child educator to learn how to foster their students to adopt a meaningful approach to learning. In this chapter, we will discuss how and why learning mindsets emerge. I contend that the Whole-Child educator can foster a growth mindset and encourage development of deep process thinking skills.

Part V is titled "Interpersonal Demonstrations of Learning and Thinking." This last chapter of the book is structured around the question: "How Do Learners Demonstrate Well-Being and Emotional Intelligence?" This part and chapter 11 will explore the many ways students can demonstrate competency in social and emotional skills. Demonstrating these skills provides educators with a bellwether of the effectiveness of their social and emotional skill teaching. Finally, the afterword proposes how administrators might go about developing and implementing a Whole-Child initiative in their district.

I

Whether to Reform or Transform, That Is the Question

How Did American Education Get Stuck, and How Do We Find Our Way Out of the Quagmire We Are In?

Chapter One

America Needs to *Transform* Rather Than *Reform* Education

> *Progress is impossible without change, and those who cannot change their minds cannot change anything.*—George Bernard Shaw

WHAT'S WRONG WITH AMERICAN EDUCATION?

The current education reform framework is based on what was once a valid, yet now outdated, nineteenth-century framework for learning and thinking. This framework not only transformed the means whereby knowledge is obtained but defined what could be known in the first place. What was construed as "real" was reduced to only that which could be observed, quantified, and reduced to simple "parts."

The nineteenth-century Industrial Revolution further impacted Western culture in another way—the rise of consumerism. This framework determined what knowledge and skills children were required to master. These changes elevated the importance of the *rational, logical, and computational* strengths of the left brain while relegating those of the right brain to the artists, poets, and musicians. Nonetheless, our understanding of how we need to think and learn has changed immensely since that time.

One of the major problems in education today is that *we do not educate the way we sense the world*. That is, we do not teach students in the same manner that they experience life in their everyday world. Toward that end, the belief that has been portrayed is that American education has lost its way. Moreover, it is losing its high international educational ranking in virtually every significant measure. At the center of this disconnect is that traditional education is organized into disciplines that deal with a specific type of knowledge as separate subjects. These discrete disciplines created the illusion that one can only gain knowledge, and therefore understanding, through mastery of those disciplines.

This assumption deluded us into thinking we could eventually amass knowledge by dissecting and reducing the world into its most elemental components. Such misleading thinking has led to, among other things, our current global ecological crisis. Mary Kennedy (1992) asserted that American students are not developing competency in higher-level thinking and reasoning processes.

Additionally, this mindset has left us with a view of reality bereft of *purpose, meaning, and value*. Further compounding our "left-brain," discipline-based approach to learning is that we undervalue "meaning." Some educational researchers assert that teachers' view of learning appears primarily to be information-based rather than meaning-based. Moreover, they maintain it is now crucial to transform teachers' views of teaching from instructionist to constructivist approaches to learning and thinking.

Educational achievement is assessed on a national level with the National Assessment of Educational Progress (NAEP)—also known as the "Nation's Report Card." The NAEP measures achievement in science, mathematics, and other subjects of American fourth-, eighth-, and twelfth-grade students. A recent analysis (Palmer et al., 2010) of NAEP results revealed the following percentages of high school seniors *not proficient* in:

- Critical Thinking: 89 percent;
- Reading Level 2: 55 percent;
- Writing Level 3: 72 percent; and
- Math Level 3: 82 percent.

Moreover, Lindholm et al. (2005) conducted a study investigating the percent of high school seniors who scored *below* the college readiness benchmarks for English composition, algebra, social sciences, and biology. The results of students by race/ethnicity were:

- Asian American: 71 percent;
- Caucasian: 74 percent;
- American Indian: 90 percent;
- Hispanic: 91 percent;
- African American: 97 percent; and
- all students: 79 percent.

Therefore, a majority of high school seniors from *any race or ethnicity* were found not to be college ready. However, the picture is even bleaker when American students are assessed among themselves relative to previous years. The latest NAEP assessment results revealed there has been no progress in either mathematics or reading. Furthermore, the lowest-performing students are doing even more poorly and have not shown any progress over the past thirty years (Sparks, 2016).

In summary, today's U.S. classrooms suffer from depth of understanding issuing from too much lecture-based teaching. Furthermore, what is obviously lacking is development of deep processing and reasoning abilities.

American students are also compared on an international scale with the Trends in International Mathematics and Science Study (TIMSS) and Program for International Student Assessment (PISA). TIMSS assesses mathematics and science achievement among fourth- and eighth-grade students, and PISA assesses mathematics, science, and reading literacy among fifteen-year-olds. Both standardized assessments provide educators with an index of how American students fare in comparison to their international peers.

American fifteen-year-olds did not perform significantly better in science or reading on the PISA in 2015 compared with the results in previous years. However, their math performance considerably declined since 2012 and 2009, which were the last two times PISA was administered. These results ranked the United States roughly in the middle of international education systems in reading and science on PISA but below average in math (Sparks, 2016). Overall, the United States ranked fourteenth out of the top fourteen nations in both the 2015 TIMSS and PISA results.

Singapore, Japan, and the Republic of Korea led all nations as they have in previous years (Sparks, 2016). Moreover, many other nations have consistently outperformed their American counterparts in international assessments. Therefore, the results of these assessments are an indictment of American education as being inferior to most other developed nations. American schools' continued adherence to an outmoded way of thinking and learning has ill-prepared today's youth for tomorrow's challenges.

Moreover, this outmoded thinking has also promoted mediocrity by squelching *creativity, innovative thinking, and nonconformity*. These were the hallmark characteristics responsible for our nation's rise as a major global economic leader. President Barack Obama challenged America's educators to place high expectations and foster high performance in today's students because far too many schools do not meet these standards.

> Maintaining our leadership in research and technology is crucial to America's success. But if we want to win the future—if we want innovation to produce jobs in America and not overseas—then we also have to win the race to educate our kids. . . . When a child walks into a classroom, it should be a place of high expectations and high performance. But too many schools don't meet this test. (Obama, 2011)

Today's global society leaves the American student at a disadvantage that can only be remedied by a significant change in the way we structure and approach teaching and learning. In the July 10, 2010, *Newsweek* article "The Creativity Crisis," the point was made that while America is moving more toward high-stakes testing, the rest of the world (e.g., India, China, and Singapore) is moving in the other direction. Moreover, contrary to America, they are increasing an emphasis on creativity and "whole-brain," real-world skills (Bronson & Merryman, 2010). Singapore's minister of education states:

> One of the key adjustments under way is in the way we educate our young so as to develop in them a willingness to keep learning, and an ability to experiment, innovate, and take risks. . . . Our ability to create and innovate will be Singapore's most important asset in [the] future. (Wagner, 2008, pp. 76–77)

This innovative educational philosophy is also readily observed in the highly successful educational systems of Finland, South Korea, Hong Kong/China, and Japan. Many educators disagree with and are critical of an increased reliance on testing (Wexler, 2018). We can learn how to move forward by following China's lead. China now requires every school from K–12 through college to teach entrepreneurial skills to produce and foster the development of creativity while de-emphasizing high-stake tests (Wagner, 2012).

It is, therefore, ironic that

> U.S. employers rate *creativity/innovation* among the top five skills that will increase in importance over the next five years, and *stimulating innovation/creativity* and *enabling entrepreneurship* is among the top 10 challenges of U.S. CEO's. (italics mine, Lichtenberg & Wright, 2008, p. 1)

Therefore, it is clear that our mission is to promote the systemic change requisite to restore American educational performance as the vanguard to which other nations will seek to aspire.

> Today, schools have the potential to stand as the great incubators and accelerators of our democracy, places where skills can be learned and ideas shared within a building—and immediately exported to the wider world through the voices of the students . . . but they must also adapt to the seismic shifts that have resulted from the revolution in communication technology (Moran, 2006, p. 82).

TEST, TEST, TEST: THE FLAW IN THE VISION

Unfortunately, the national movement to create standards-based assessments rather than those that evaluate procedural skills has become the dictum for assessing teacher effectiveness. The belief is that if it can't be put into measurable terms, then it is useless to rely on it to evaluate either students or educators. This thinking led to the development of a reliance on the use of "high-stakes" standardized testing.

These tests were designed to assess both the academic proficiency of American students, as well as the competency of their educators.

> Over the past decade, the high-stakes testing regime has squeezed out much of the curriculum that can make schools an engaging and enriching experience for students, and teachers have been forced to dilute their creativity to teach to the test. (Walker, 2014, p. 2)

A review (Supovitz, 2009) of the efficacy of high-stakes testing revealed that:

1. educators have been forced to offer a narrow curriculum experience that is lacking in depth due to extended periods of test preparation (teaching to the test);
2. while the high-stakes results are useful to policymakers, they are insufficient in providing classroom teachers with insight with respect to informing or remediating individual students' academic performance;
3. standardized tests have widened the academic performance gap between white and non-white students (Ritt & Maddolyn, 2016);
4. standardized tests have fostered future test takers at the expense of developing critical thinking (Ritt & Maddolyn, 2016);
5. standardized tests are unreliable and cannot be interpreted without considering personal and family characteristics that impact a child's learning (e.g., mental health, family relationships, violence, etc.) (Apple, 2006);
6. educators spend an inordinate amount of time prepping for standardized tests, but there is no evidence from the NAEP that the time spent on tests enhances academic performance (Zernike, 2015); and
7. educators have less time to focus on developing higher-order thinking skills (Darling-Hammond, 2007). Furthermore, "high-stakes" tests have proven themselves incapable of assessing the essential critical skills and knowledge requisite to be "college and career" ready (American College Test [ACT], 2010, 2011; Amrein & Berliner, 2003; Barnes & Slate, 2011; Symonds, Schwartz, & Ferguson, 2011; Zhao, 2006, 2009a, 2009b).

What the reformers are oblivious to are the skills and characteristics required to be successful learners and workers. These characteristics include *competency in using cognitive and metacognitive learning strategies to self-regulate and take a meaningful approach to learning.* However, none of these can be easily measured by standardized tests. The cry from classroom educators that "students are more than a test score" states the obvious flaw in the standardized testing agenda of the American education reform effort. This is the central issue when it comes to the current state of evaluating both students' and educators' performance.

There are certain explicit and measurable factors that successful educators possess. Nonetheless, effective teaching also requires *creating a learning environment conducive to motivating students to want to learn.* However, none of these can be checked off on administrators' evaluation rubric. Additionally, isn't it ironic that there is a lack of dialogue between those who want to reform education and those who actually educate our nation's children?

The Obama administration's ESSA is a response to the failed promises of NCLB and Race to the Top. Every Student Succeeds Act (ESSA) legislation returned more responsibility for raising standards, expectations, and performance for both students and educators. Nonetheless, like its predecessors, it consists of flawed assumptions regarding unrealistic expectations for all students. Furthermore, the mandate to assess learning based on the Common Core State Standards (CCSS) represents an incongruous, if not illogical, alignment of expectations. The underlying assumption of CCSS and ESSA misses that students not only do not learn at the same pace but also have different capacities and motivations to learn.

WHO'S TO BLAME FOR THE UNDERACHIEVEMENT OF AMERICAN STUDENTS?

Corporate America has convinced political leaders that American schools are not only failing but are doing so primarily because educators are not holding their students accountable to high academic standards. However, it isn't that educators are not challenging their students. Rather it is unrealistic to expect all students can and should be able to achieve the same level of academic expectation. Teachers have had to resort to teaching all students the same standards-based curriculum. Thus the "one size fits all" is designed to level the academic "playing field."

It is an implicitly understood goal that teachers seek to provide the *same* learning opportunities to all students in order for them to perform well on standardized tests. Compounding the shortsightedness of this mindset are overcrowded classrooms that are increasingly populated with children from disadvantaged backgrounds. These children are more likely than children from affluent backgrounds to lack parental support and commitment that ensures they come to school prepared to learn. Additionally, today's classroom educators have to contend with an increasing amount of social and emotional issues.

Children are intrinsically curious and love to learn. So why are many students unmotivated and failing? It is a premise of this book that the current educational system is flawed in its fundamental assumptions and philosophy. Our current educational mindset has a system fault that is responsible for failing our kids. Achievement requires students to be motivated to learn and spend the necessary time and effort to accomplish learning goals. However, while motivation is an internal drive, providing students with stimulating learning experiences is the means to get and keep them engaged and on task. *It is high time that educational leaders recognize that students have unique learning needs and skills. Therefore, personalized learning strategies need to replace the "one size fits all."*

THE EMERGENCE OF A CULTURE OF LEARNING AND THINKING

The curricular needs of today's twenty-first-century school learners are no longer anything remotely resembling that of their parents, let alone grandparents. Rather, the schools of today and tomorrow need to embrace a new *culture of learning and thinking*. In this new *culture*, the learning process will morph from the static twentieth-century structure to a dynamic twenty-first-century system that constantly responds to change. Ironically, the relentless pace of change that is responsible for society's disequilibrium is also the source of humankind's greatest hope.

The emergence of social media platforms has transformed how we learn, live, work, shop, play, and even meet others. The growing digital, networked infrastructure is amplifying our ability to access and use nearly unlimited resources. Simultaneously, the networked system keeps people connected; thereby creating ever-expanding pathways to deep, expansive personal learning. This new type of learning is a *cultural phenomenon* that underlies a large number of students' experiences.

This new type of learning takes place without traditional textbooks, credentialed instructors, and classrooms. It requires environments that are bounded yet provides complete freedom of action within these boundaries. The digital age has ushered in a new way to live, work, play, and educate. President Obama (Obama, 2011) eloquently conceptualized this in his 2011 State of the Union address:

> None of us can predict with certainty what the next big industry will be, or where the new jobs will come from. . . . What we can do—what America does

better than anyone—is spark the creativity and imagination of our people. . . . In America, innovation doesn't just change our lives. It's how we make a living.

Humanity has reached a point in its cultural evolution whereby progressing forward into an unknown future is no longer dependent upon *disciplinary thinking*. Rather we now recognize that survival in the twenty-first century and beyond is dependent upon understanding the importance of *interdisciplinary thinking*. We now live in a global community characterized by a web of relationships between myriad social, political, economic, and ecological processes.

TODAY'S STUDENTS NEED DIFFERENT SKILLS TO THRIVE IN THE TWENTY-FIRST CENTURY

Howard Gardner, Tony Wagner, and Ken Robinson have persuasively argued that the skills and abilities kids need today to succeed are very different than those of just a generation ago. Whole-Child educational thinkers maintain that we need to provide opportunities for today's students to feel comfortable developing a new set of skills—*social and emotional skills in addition to their reasoning, analytical, and communicative skills*. If we don't foster these skills, we are not only doing them a disservice but also failing to prepare them for *career and college success*.

It is here where technology can be of use in providing learners with authentic contexts to problem solve, use their imagination, and be innovative in their solutions. Digital technology has forever changed the way we communicate, think, and learn and, as such, has transformed "classroom" teaching. No longer are educators "trapped" within the four walls of their classrooms to teach. Rather the Internet has placed the world literally at our fingertips. Students seeking to learn more about European art can virtually visit European libraries and museums. Science students can Skype with experts and actively dialogue with others across the world as they participate in online webcasts.

In his book *The World Is Flat*, Thomas Friedman revealed that we are no longer limited spatially and temporally from others. Through the Internet, the world is at one's disposal to learn from and share information. Beginning with the oral traditions through the inventions of writing, photography, telegraphy, phones, radio, television, and computers, every new advance in information technology has increased the ability to communicate with others. This is attributed to increasing the "bandwidth" and "signal strength" of the information. Together they serve to reach a wider range of individuals while reducing the time and space that kept us isolated from others.

The time has come for educational reformers to acknowledge that the skill set needed for college and career success today has changed since they were students in traditional classrooms. Therefore, what is needed today, more than ever, is a shift in the way we understand what today's youth need to be able to *imagine, create, and innovate* fresh ways of living and working. This shift will ensure and sustain prosperity for all Americans.

If we stay on the linear path to learning vis-à-vis the "one size fits all" design, we can forget about graduating independent, creative thinkers. This country needs a new breed of learners who will take their place in the workplace to keep America strong as an innovative nation. The root of the word "education" is the word *educere*, which means to "draw out." However, the thrust of the "one size fits all" reform agenda views education as a process of "pouring in" information.

Therefore, what has been ongoing over the past few decades are attempts at restoring America's education system to what it once was. The problem is that returning to what we were is moving backward. Obviously, these *reform* efforts haven't changed the underlying beliefs that held sway throughout the twentieth century. Merriam-Webster's online dictionary defines the difference between *reform* and *transform* as follows: *reform* is to "put into a new and improved form or condition; to amend or improve by change of form or removal of faults or abuses"; while *transform* is to "change in composition or structure, to change in character or condition."

Embracing a Whole-Child approach to teaching and learning is the most recent outgrowth of the progressive educational ethos. Ted Christou (2012, p. 61) cites three aims of progressive education that are central to Whole-Child teaching:

1. focus on the individual learner's aptitudes and interests rather than upon a rigid curriculum developed in a bygone age;
2. engage the learner actively in the construction of knowledge, a process prohibited by the memorization and examination of content; and
3. commit to relating school life to the modern world and its concerns, not to the affairs of a world of the past. Therefore, the progressive educator focuses on adapting teaching strategies to address the needs of the whole child.

Nehring (2006) eloquently defined the difference between the progressive learner-centered movement and the traditional school-centered one as follows: "Progressive schools are the legacy of a long and proud tradition of thoughtful school practice stretching back for centuries"—including hands-on learning, multiage classrooms, and mentor-apprentice relationships—while what we generally refer to as traditional schooling "is largely the result of outdated policy changes that have calcified into conventions" (p. 32).

These aims still apply to learning in the twenty-first century. The difference lies in preparing the whole child for the very different global landscape students are immersed in today. Therefore, the current Whole-Child approach is actually the third wave of progressive education. In an article entitled "Progressive Education: Why It's Hard to Beat, but Also Hard to Find," Alfie Kohn (2015) cites the core aims of modern progressive education that lie at the heart of the Whole-Child approach to teaching:

1. addressing the social, emotional, and cognitive needs of the *whole child*;
2. creating a learning *community* among students to create a caring, safe, and validating place to learn;
3. fostering *collaboration* with an emphasis on problem-solving;
4. embracing *social justice* whereby responsibility of actions toward others isn't limited to the classroom but also in their everyday relationships with others;
5. fostering *intrinsic motivation* whereby learners adopt an internal predilection to learn and a growth mindset;
6. fostering *deep understanding*, or what is referred to as meaningful learning, by adopting constructivist pedagogies that require use of higher-order process thinking skills and deep reflection;
7. fostering *active learning* whereby students are part of a dialogue with each other and their facilitator and therefore learning emerges as this process flows through constant construction rather than mere acquisition of the concepts typical of instructionist pedagogies; and
8. *taking kids seriously*, which means understanding the uniqueness of each child and, as such, requires adapting learning strategies that meet the learning demands of each learner. Therefore, the progressive educator welcomes going off on tangents to follow the thinking of students.

SUMMARY

Political and corporate reformers assume that the educational system of the past was optimized to meet the learning demands of the populace in the new digital age. Much to the contrary, what is needed now is to *change the form and character* of American education—*ergo, transform it*. What America needs is a new and different form of education that embraces a new *nature, condition, and function* rather than merely returning to that of the past.

The challenge for educators is to provide engaging learning opportunities whereby students transform information into knowledge and subsequently internalize it into a meaningful understanding. Therefore, in contrast to the nineteenth-century "factory" model, this book explains and defines the framework for real and effective educational transformation. This framework consists of a shift toward a more *Whole-Child process and learner-centered approach* for education.

This approach, unlike the "one size fits all" instructionist model, provides constructivist-learning opportunities for a diverse population of learners. Throughout the remainder of the book the term "teacher-centered" will be used to represent the twentieth-century traditional educator. "Learner-centered" will represent the twenty-first-century educator. *The intention of the book's theme is to provide a persuasive framework to adopt a Whole-Child approach to teaching and learning. Furthermore, this approach is designed to meet the social, emotional, and cognitive needs of learners.*

Chapter Two

Transformation Requires a Systemic Change

Without change there is no innovation, creativity, or incentive for improvement. Those who initiate change will have a better opportunity to manage the change that is inevitable. —William Pollard

NATURE OF SYSTEMS IN RESPONSE TO CHANGE

The quest for whole-school reform is not new. Schools, particularly high schools, have been the focus of reform attempts for decades (e.g., Boyer, 1983; Sizer, 1984, 1992, 1996; Lee, 2001). Nonetheless, high school reform has not been successful due to two reasons. First of all there is a historical resistance of high schools to change (Lee, 2001; McQuillan, 1998; Muncey & McQuillan, 1996; Sarason & Seymour, 1990). Secondly, reform change is ultimately dependent on key personnel (Hargreaves & Fink, 2000).

Educational reform efforts over the past few decades have not only been piecemeal but also reflective of the industrial age. However, there have been a lot of changes in the global landscape since the nineteenth century. Consequently, reform efforts have had little impact on education (Banathy, 1991). Banathy suggests five reasons why reform efforts have not brought about any significant changes to America's educational system.

Reformers' efforts:

- have been fragmentary, disconnected, and incremental;
- failed to integrate solution ideas;
- have been imposed on a discipline-by-discipline study of education;
- assumed a atomistic approach to restructure "parts" of the whole; and

- stayed within the boundaries of the existing system (not thinking out of the box).

Any effective reform requires a systemic change in the organization. Education, like all systems, has a unique behavior that is resistant to change. Nonetheless, it is able to change with small but significant influences. System theorists use the term "attractor" to describe the general tendencies a system tends to display, and return to, when perturbed by small effects. In other words, systems seem to tend toward returning to balance and stability. Systems have built-in attractors that serve to keep the system in balance despite changes imposed on them. Small disturbances or disruptions can ultimately lead to instability in a given system and influence the direction that the system may take.

System scientists refer to these disturbances as "turning points." *While turning points may create chaos in the system, they can point a system in a new direction.* Turning points can lead the system to evolve a new and emergent order of behavior. Thus, an instability in a system can lead it to transform itself with the emergence of a new attractor. *As we will see later in this chapter, in order to transform education, there needs to be a "disruption" that, if sustained, will give rise to a new "attractor" or set of behaviors.*

The American educational system needs a new vision, which therefore necessitates being *transformed* rather than merely reformed. Making a systemic change requires aligning all the interrelated components in order to function. This is especially the case for living systems. *Later I will argue that educational systems are "living systems."* Moreover, systems regulate themselves by complex feedback processes. These processes need energy to maintain their behavior.

These feedback processes serve to sustain an ecosystem. Ecosystems are stable and resist changes. Therefore, even if a fire, flood, drought, or tornado disrupts the natural cycles, in time the same ecosystem will reemerge. Nonetheless, the ecosystem *can* change, but it requires energy put into the system. Most Americans spend their weekends taking care of their green lawns and gardens and landscaping. However, left unkempt, their well-kept lawns and landscapes would soon become a meadow or a forest. *Thus, the point is to affect any real and lasting change (i.e., transformation in education), energy needs to be put into maintaining that change and all components must be aligned to sustain the new system.*

EDUCATIONAL SYSTEMS ARE "LIVING PROCESSES"

The words "living process" conjure up other words like "growth" and "development," among others. Progressive educator John Dewey said it more eloquently: "Education is not preparation for life; education is life itself" (Dewey, 1897, p. 78). Educational systems are "living processes" in the sense that their effectiveness is a function of several feedback relationships among students, teachers, and dozens of other certified and noncertified staff members.

Curricula and standards are "living processes" in the sense that they are constantly being revised and expanded and therefore constantly growing and developing. Examining the metaphor a little further, educational systems are in the business of "nourishing" and "nurturing" learners to "cultivate" the skills and knowledge to contribute the "fruits" of their labor to human society. Therefore, education systems foster the growth and development of learners. In fact, the sole raison d'être of school systems is to foster learners' cognitive, social, and emotional growth and well-being.

If plants don't receive the proper amount of sunlight, fertile soil, water, carbon dioxide, and space, they will wither and die. So goes the analogy that if learners aren't nourished and nurtured by the educational system, their intellectual, social, and/or emotional growth will be stunted. "Grow" and "develop" are verbs and therefore processes—so too is "learn." The outcome of pollination and fertilization of an apple flower is to produce apples. Educators "pollinate" and "fertilize" the minds of their students to enhance their capacity to learn, think, create, and evaluate. Moreover, the reason apple trees expend enormous amounts of energy to produce seeds is that, when germinated, the seeds give rise to new apple trees.

Therefore, knowledge is the "fruit" of the learning process. This "fruit" contains "seeds" or ideas that when "germinated" create a new symphony, a work of art, a new scientific theory, a new technology, or a best-selling novel. The labors of an educational system bring forth a change in the world, one learner at a time.

CHANGING THE SYSTEM MEANS ALIGNING ALL COMPONENTS

Recently, science educators developed a new set of K–12 science standards—Next Generation Science Standards (NGSS). NGSS is a research-based, nationwide effort to provide a rigorous K–12 context. It consists of core ideas, practices, and cross-disciplinary standards (life, physical, and earth and space sciences) for science. Science teachers across the country attended workshops to understand the well-thought-out and detailed design of NGSS.

Science teachers were also apprised of the changes they needed to make in their classroom teaching in light of the new standards. The point to make here is that the systemic change in science education did not come about overnight. Rather it took a team of experts years to develop the standards' framework. More importantly, this framework needed to be explained so teachers could incorporate it into their classroom teaching. Moreover, since the thrust of the NGSS is to present topics in problem-solving contexts, science teachers were required to change their current curricula, test questions, and laboratory activities.

In the end, if the NGSS turns out to be a more effective set of science standards, then standardized test scores should increase (i.e., TIMSS and PISA). However, in the event they don't, then teachers will need to conduct a more thorough in-house self-study to examine any issues with the rollout of the NGSS. Thus, the initial change in standards will ultimately be used to reflect on the efficacy of them in enhancing science teaching and learning.

NGSS is an example of a complex "ecological" feedback system that requires ongoing monitoring of the impact of new standards. In this case, the various interrelated components include: the standards, teachers, pedagogies, curricula, laboratory equipment, students, tests, laboratory exercises, and workshops. While these new standards impact K–12 science practices, skills, and competencies, they only impact science classes. *Therefore, what is needed to maintain transformational change in education is a constant supply of energy, resources, and monitoring to maintain the new changes.*

WHAT IS NEEDED TODAY IS A SYSTEMIC TRANSFORMATION IN EDUCATION

A *transformational change* in education is needed to adapt to the new demands of learning in the twenty-first century. Transformation requires a systemic change. Smith and O'Day's (1991) definition of "systemic" was adopted by the U.S. Department of Education.

Systemic change in education:

- includes creating high achievement expectations for all students who are encouraged and supported in developing understanding of a set of standards;
- requires aligning the educational standards with all aspects of the teaching and learning process; and
- involves fostering dialogue and decision making between all individuals involved in the education enterprise.

Lusi (1997, p. 6) defines systemic educational change:

- It *"strives to reform the education system as a system"* (italics in original). That means education systems' component policies need to be coherent across the system.
- Systemic reform unequivocally endeavors to support school-site efforts at redesigning educational programs in support of all students. "Top-down" and ad hoc fiats are insufficient. Schools and districts must be supported to transform teaching and learning as part of a coherent redesign.

Institutional change typically occurs from the top down. However, institutions are too complex for this type of reform to effect any lasting change on them. Change that is lasting and self-sustaining must be transformational and, as such, requires a whole-system change. Every facet of the institution needs to be considered. Moreover, for change to be impactful and lasting all concerned parties need to "buy in" to the changes. The leadership may have a terrific plan but if the rank and file does not embrace the new design, then the plan will fail. Therefore, transformational change needs to be carefully and thoroughly conceived together with representatives of all concerned parties.

THE ROLE OF DISRUPTION IN SYSTEMIC CHANGE

It is clear that American education has changed neither its infrastructure (e.g., independent classrooms, teaching in batches) nor its discipline-based framework since the industrial age. The times have changed as we now have left behind the industrial age of the nineteenth and twentieth centuries and entered the digital age of the twenty-first century. With that change has come the need for schools to develop a new set of skills in today's citizens. Toward this end, education systems need to make the shift from a *school-centric* approach to a *student-centric* approach to learning and thinking.

However, making this shift requires more than just deciding to make the change. Rather what is needed is a disruption in the way things are done. In *Disrupting Class: How Disruptive Innovation Will Change the Way the World Learns*, Christensen et al. (2016) define a disruption as "a positive force. It is the process by which an innovation transforms a market whose services or products are complicated and expensive into one where simplicity, convenience, accessibility, and affordability characterize the industry" (p. 11).

All systems are characterized by inertia to keep doing the same thing they were designed to do. Therefore, it is difficult to change a system. Nonetheless, as discussed above, even a small change can potentially create an instability in the system that if sustained will change its behavior. The disruption creates a "branching point" whereby the "old" and "new" behaviors may coexist for a while. If the "new" path is sustained and grows in strength, then it will, in time, displace the "old" path, thereby changing the behavior of the system. Therefore, by analogy, "instability" is what Christensen et al. refer to as a "disruption" and, as such, is a change that can potentially change the entire system.

Christensen et al. (2016) ask: what is the incentive to change from a *school-centric* to a *student-centric* approach to learning? They chose *computer technology* as one major way school systems can usher in an innovative change to create a *student-centric* approach to learning and thinking. While computer use in schools has been a staple for many years, they have typically been used to supplement rather than change the traditional style to teaching. The predominant way teachers have used computers is to remediate students or serve as a resource for teachers to present their lessons.

In contrast, a *student-centric* use of computers could potentially be designed to "tailor-make" the content to suit the specific type of learning style for each student. The difference is a shift from what Christensen et al. (2016) refers to as a "monolithic technology" to a *student-centric* technology. The former is characterized by a single instructional approach used to teach each student in the same manner or supplement using the same textbook. In contrast, a modular student-centric technology provides students with the curricular content in distinctive ways dependent upon how they learn.

Since learners learn in different ways, the *student-centric* approach seems more educationally sound than a monolithic one. All systems, particularly if they are human-based, tend to do what they do because they have always done things that way. In order to change them, the behavior of systems needs to overcome their inherent tendency to resist change—*the inertia to stay the course.*

COMPUTER-BASED LEARNING (CBL) AS A DISRUPTIVE FORCE IN EDUCATION

Therefore, why won't school systems change to suit a new era? It is far easier to change a system if its components are modular rather than interdependent. The first computer systems consisted of interdependent processors. If one failed, the system failed. However, as computer technology evolved, its components became modular, and consequently components could be outsourced to a variety of companies that produce a single component.

Modularity enabled customization. Moreover, if one component failed, you could just replace the component. Such was the case with Dell computers, which replaced the older (Digital Equipment Corporation) computer design. Dell could now tailor make a computer for each customer in forty-eight hours. For educational systems to change requires not merely viewing and using technology in a new and modular way. Rather the new technology must be shown to enhance the process it seeks to improve—*learning.*

Education guru Howard Gardner defines intelligence as "the ability to solve problems that one encounters in real life; the ability to generate new problems to solve and the ability to make something or offer a service that is valued within one's culture" (Campbell, Campbell, & Dickenson, 2004, p. 76).

In his landmark book *Multiple Intelligences,* Gardner (1993) determined there exist at least eight separate forms of intelligence including:

1. naturalist intelligence,
2. musical intelligence,
3. logical-mathematical intelligence,
4. existential intelligence,
5. interpersonal intelligence,
6. bodily-kinesthetic intelligence,
7. linguistic intelligence, and
8. intra-personal intelligence.

Schools typically only address a few of these, predominantly linguistic and logic-mathematical intelligences. Moreover, learners learn at different paces. Some need more time than others to reflect on and process information. Therefore, in a *school-centric* monolithic approach, all learners have to learn the way a teacher teaches at the same pace regardless of their learning style and pace at which they learn best. A student-centric approach to learning and thinking might be more effective in addressing most, if not all, of these intelligences.

This approach aligns the learning approach with the learner rather than the learner having to adapt to the learning approach. *Thus, the question now becomes: how can schools adopt a student-centric design to teach batches of students with a standardized curriculum in an effective and efficient manner?*

K–12 technology guru Larry Cuban (2000; 2001) argues that while criticism of the use of technology is pervasive, it typically gets used merely to maintain rather than transform learning. Christensen et al. (2016) offer computer-based learning (CBL) as a learning approach that can disrupt and open up the current system to new paths toward educating students. Regarding this, CBL can remove the constraints imposed on learners in the current monolithic approach to education. One use of CBL is to offer schools the option of providing online courses for which there are too few students or too little funding to assign a teacher to teach them.

However, the real game-changer use of CBL is the growing development of interactive e-learning software that monitors and detects students' learning patterns. This software infers students' learning preferences and predicts what sequence of learning tasks will optimize learning a concept (Paramythis & Loidl-Reisinger, 2004). Thus, *adaptive learning* software scaffolds and differentiates the sequence of learning tasks according to the learning behavior of the student. Some interactive adaptive learning software programs have innovative algorithms to aid learners in discovering solutions to problems (Brusilovsky, 1999).

Moreover, since students learn in different ways and at different paces, adaptive learning software personalizes the learning needs of each student. Adaptive learning software is well-suited for homebound or home-schooled students.

Christensen et al. (2016) discuss how entire courses might be offered to students in the digital space of computer software. Virtual ChemLab is an online course that currently offers a complete (laboratory activities included) high school chemistry course. The advantage is that all the principles and activities normally conducted or prohibited in a four-walled chemistry classroom can be performed using just this software. To date more than 150,000 students across the country have used the program.

Of course, using CBL does not preclude having teachers. In a CBL approach to teaching and learning, the role of the teacher transforms from what Harvard educator Tony Wagner calls the "sage on the stage to the guide on the side" (Wagner, 2012, p. 241). This new role of the teacher takes the form of a one-on-one facilitator, coach, or mentor for each student. Thus, rather than using computers as tools to demonstrate learning or remediate learners, new dynamic educational software can serve as a unique path to learning in the way each learner learns best.

Student-centric software can be designed so that students can only move forward once they master course content. Therefore, administering summative assessments is no longer necessary. The advantage to using interactive CBL software is to allow the learner to pace their learning and receive continuous and personalized formative feedback on their progress.

PROJECT-BASED LEARNING AS A DISRUPTIVE FORCE IN EDUCATION

Project-based learning (PBL) is another innovative disruptive approach to learning and thinking. PBL "is a student driven, teacher-facilitated approach to learning. Learners pursue knowledge by asking questions that have piqued their natural curiosity" (Bell, 2010, p. 39).

Teachers serve the role as guide and mentor to aide each student in developing a project that investigates his or her question(s). Students may also work collaboratively with others who have similar questions. PBL projects foster self-regulation because each project must be carefully planned, conducted, and written up.

Thus, PBL personalizes learning while fostering collaboration and communication with other students on real-world issues or problems. Effectively communicating is an essential skill and one that PBL develops naturally by fostering collaboration between learners. Self-regulation, personalized learning, and collaboration are all essential twenty-first-century educational skills. PBL is also interdisciplinary in that students' projects may draw from problems issuing from math, science, social sciences, or the arts and humanities. Each student is held accountable for his or her work to a greater extent in a PBL framework than in a traditional classroom.

PBL also fosters independent learning and thinking on a project of their own choosing, thereby serving to increase the intrinsic motivation to learn. Unlike traditional assignments, students engaged in PBL projects follow their own interests and pursue deep rather than superficial learning. Deep learning requires use of high-order thinking skills.

Standardized test scores reveal that students engaged in PBL projects outscore their traditionally educated peers (Geier et al., 2008) particularly with respect to procedural questions that used formulas (Boaler, 1999). Gultekin (2005) reports that the "project-based learning approach improves academic success, makes learning enjoyable, meaningful and permanent, and develops essential and important skills in students" (p. 553).

PBL is a constructivist approach to problem solving (constructivism will be discussed at length in chapter 6) in that every aspect of the project emerges from learners constructing meaning. Thus both CBL and PBL provide educators with a way to transform the *one size fit all* to *one-on-one* mentoring. Both approaches provide learners with a personalized way to pace their own learning and foster initiative, intrinsic motivation, and self-regulation. Moreover, they free up the teacher to spend more time talking *with* students as mentors and coaches rather than talking *at* them from the front of the room.

In the end, both CBL and PBL *student-centric* approaches provide opportunities for learners to stay motivated and engaged in meaningful learning activities. In the next section, we will explore the efforts under way to develop a *student-centric* approach to teaching the whole child.

PLACE-BASED EDUCATION (PBE) AS A DISRUPTIVE FORCE IN EDUCATION

The philosophical foundations underlying place-based-education have been around for quite some time. Progressive educator John Dewey (1897) believed you could not separate learning from experience. Dewey eloquently defined education "as a process of living not a preparation for future living" (p. 1). Gruenewald (2003) more directly tied Dewey's thinking to actual schooling: "Place-conscious education, therefore, aims to work against the isolation of schooling's discourses and practices from the living world outside the increasingly placeless institution of schooling" (p. 620).

There is a qualitative difference between learning concepts in a classroom context and experiencing them firsthand in their natural context. The former is not genuine whereas the latter is authentic. Learning in authentic contexts is the basis of situated learning. In their seminal paper, Seely-Brown et al. (1989) argued that you couldn't isolate knowledge as it is learned from how it is used. For instance, the concept of a hammer is qualitatively distinct and incomplete if only known by name rather than its use. Moreover, if new uses are made for a hammer, an understanding of these new usages only can be gained when used in the new context.

Seely-Brown et al. reasoned that learning and cognition are situated in specific contexts: "The activity in which knowledge is developed and deployed, is not separable from or ancillary to learning and cognition. . . . Rather it is an integral part of what is learned. . . . Learning and cognition . . . are fundamentally situated" (p. 32).

Seely-Brown et al. maintain there is a distinct difference between how a concept is taught in a classroom compared to doing so in an authentic, real-world context. Thus, the meaning students develop in either context is qualitatively, if not quantitatively, different. Learning in authentic contexts is characteristic of apprenticeships where the apprentice becomes proficient in the actual practices and interactions of a specific craft or trade. For instance, you wouldn't want a carpenter or electrician working on your house if they either had only read about the skills in a book or had learned them on their own.

Situated cognition is about teaching in authentic contexts or at least problem solving in the cultural "space" in which the concepts are actually used. Teaching a science lesson situated in the culture of thinking like a scientist (e.g., experimenting using scientific methods) would be more authentic than merely teaching the concepts in a vacuum. However, an even more authentic example would be to take a field trip to an actual laboratory and speak with scientists about how to "do" science.

This is the importance of place-based education (PBE). PBE extends learning beyond the four walls of the classroom and provides students with opportunities to work on community-based issues. PBE offers students novel ways of knowing, seeing, and experiencing the world (Baldwin et al., 2017). PBE takes students out of the classroom and places them in authentic real-world contexts. David Sobel (2004) defined PBE as "the process of using the local community and environment as a starting point to teach concepts in language arts, mathematics, social studies, science and other subjects across the curriculum" (p. 4).

PBE provides students with opportunities to engage in real problems. Moreover, Antioch educator David Sobel (1999) maintains that PBE affords learners with opportunities to explore natural environments and issues associated with them (e.g., global warming, endangered species). Moreover, when lessons provide students with authentic contexts, they develop a deeper appreciation of natural environments.

Lowenstein and Smith (2017) wrote about the significant PBE that educator Laurette Rogers and her fourth-grade class experienced that led them to create the Students and Teachers Restoring a Watershed (STRAW) program in California. Rogers had learned that freshwater shrimp were being affected by the streamside denuding of its banks by grazing cattle and sheep. Therefore, they studied the natural ecosystem of the shrimp and the niche they occupied in that ecosystem.

Afterward they undertook measures ensuring that future bank degradation was held in check by planting willows and other indigenous species along the creek's banks. However, their PBE didn't stop there. Rather, students from Rogers's class went to Washington and lobbied senators about supporting this type of ecological restoration in other locales. Since STRAW was conceived, forty thousand students have engaged in restoring thirty-five miles of creek embankment, as well as other wetlands.

Lowenstein and Smith (2017) also discussed the PBE of two Michigan schools. One was an urban school in Ypsilanti while the other was a private school in Ann Arbor. Two environmentally conscious organizations—SEMIS Coalition and We Are The Forest—worked with the students to assess the existing status of their school grounds' ecosystem and develop strategies to remediate any environmental issues.

PBE centers on real problem-solving opportunities and therefore provides students with learning opportunities they never could experience in a classroom. Moreover, such experiences require students to use higher-order thinking skills. Additionally, they provide students with an appreciation of their local habitats. Lowenstein and Smith (2017) cite research studies that support the significant impact PBE has on "academic performance, ecological literacy and civic capacity" (p. 55). PBE activities place students within the environs and as members of the local community.

Learning in authentic contexts changes the way both teacher and student perceives themselves and the learning process as well. Lane-Zucker (2005) commented on the unique learning opportunities offered by PBEs:

> Place based education challenges the meaning of education by asking seemingly simple questions: Where am I? What is the nature of this place? What sustains this community? . . . They are able to position themselves, imagina-

tively and actually, within the continuum of nature and culture within that place. They become part of the community, rather than passive observers of it. (p. iii)

PBE takes education to a new level by situating learners in real-world and therefore authentic contexts. The world becomes their classroom and, as such, invigorates the discussion of what normally would be discussed in their classrooms. Learners work on real issues and become motivated to effect real change. This is something they rarely are able to do in a traditional classroom setting.

PBE also makes learners realize they are members of a community and, through their actions, can make a real difference for others. Hence, something lost in modern education is now fostered with PBE—civic responsibility—which is an invaluable characteristic of eventually becoming a voting citizen. *Therefore PBE along with CBL and PBL are three disruptive forces to usher in a change in education.*

Perhaps the most recent disruptive force to education has been contending with ways to provide an effective educational process as a consequence of the impact of COVID-19. While this is by no means a concern exclusive to American classrooms, it is one that has presented major challenges for even the most intrepid and dedicated educator.

Throughout the country, teachers have been forced to adapt their teaching methods and assignments. They have had to resort to teaching in either a virtual or hybrid "classroom" environment. Teaching online presents itself as a far more challenging task than in-person teaching. Nonetheless, many innovative educators discovered the silver lining in the dark cloud of COVID protocols and developed new strategies to teach in this disruptive climate.

COVID teaching has forced teachers to capitalize on the virtual space by utilizing computer-based programs and project-based learning assignments. Many of the software programs used in the virtual space can easily be used to create breakout groups of students so they can work together using Google Docs, Makers Empire, Drawp for School, and Minecraft: Education Edition, to name a few. While the COVID pandemic has created challenges for educators, the new strategies developed because of it will surely impact educational praxis post-COVID.

If we consider that different educational systems provide a unique *orientating map* that educators "read" to teach learners, then the major difference between different orienting maps is how they may be used to "navigate" across different "terrains." To make this more familiar, *school-centered* teachers will "read" different orienting maps from those used by *student-centric* ones.

The difference between these two "maps" can more adroitly be illustrated with an old poem. The following John Godfrey Saxe's nineteenth-century poem is believed to be an adaptation of an old Indian parable called "The Blind Men and the Elephant" (Saxe, 1872, p. 260). The poem concerns six wise but also blind men who came across an elephant and tried to determine its shape.

> Six wise men of India
> An elephant did find
> And carefully they felt its shape
> (For all of them were blind).
> The first he felt towards the tusk,
> "It does to me appear,
> This marvel of an elephant
> Is very like a spear."
> The second sensed the creature's side
> Extended flat and tall.
> "Ahah!" he cried and did conclude,
> "This animal's a wall."
> The third had reached towards a leg
> And said, "It's clear to me
> What we should all have instead
> This creature's like a tree."
> The fourth had come upon the trunk
> Which he did seize and shake.
> Quoth he, "This so-called elephant
> Is really just a snake."
> The fifth had felt the creature's ear
> And fingers o'er it ran.
> "I have the answer, never fear,
> The creature's like a fan!"
> The sixth had come upon the tail
> As blindly he did grope.
> "Let my conviction now prevail
> This creature's like a rope."
> And so these men of missing sight
> Each argued loud and long.
> Though each was partly in the right
> They all were in the wrong.

The story of the six blind men only perceiving a part of the whole is analogous to the current *school-centric approach*, which views learning as a fragmented set of knowledge constructs divided up into separate and independent disciplines. On the other hand, the holistic observer, who sees the entire elephant, is analogous to the *student-centric approach*. The holistic observer views the parts in the context of a whole. System theory scientists have determined that all systems are composed of interdependent "parts" that interact to form an integrated "whole." Systems are, therefore, "ecological" and holistic in their reality, design, and behavior. Societies and schools may therefore be seen as "ecological" systems composed of *integrated relationships* among people, processes, beliefs, and structures.

SUMMARY

This chapter argued to transform rather than merely reform education. The former requires a systemic change while the latter only partially changes the system. Systems tend to resist change and remain stable over time. A systemic change requires disruptions that provide new perspectives and innovative ways of thinking. Some of the innovative disruptions impacting education today are computer-based learning (CBL), project-based learning (PBL), and place-based education (PBE).

In CBL, innovative computer software programs offer students personalized learning opportunities. In PBL, teachers serve as coaches to facilitate students' learning how to problem solve with a project of their own choice. PBE provides students with real-life problems in authentic contexts. All three are learner-centered approaches that offer students authentic learning experiences that promote the development of deep processing skills like critical thinking and problem solving. These and other disruptive forces in education are needed to make a shift from a school-centric to a learner-centric framework for teaching and learning.

Chapter Three

Transforming Education: The Whole-Child Paradigm

> *Education is an art—it must speak to the child's experience. To educate the whole child, his heart and his will must be reached, as well as his mind.*
> —Rudolf Steiner

WHAT'S A PARADIGM?

So what is the new framework that this book will offer to consider? Humans are storytellers and, as such, interpret experiences from a narrative perspective. While we can't foretell the future, humans can reflect on the past and attempt to find trends and explanations to better predict the future. However, these are merely stories and may not accurately forecast coming events. Much of what we think, create, and know is based upon the unique perspective of our culture's worldview, hereafter referred to as a *paradigm*.

Scientist and philosopher Thomas Kuhn (1962) coined the word "paradigm" in his seminal text *The Structure of Scientific Revolutions*. A paradigm represents the underlying assumptions and beliefs that prescribe how to create meaning from experience. Physicist and philosopher Fritjof Capra (1996) further defined the meaning of a paradigm in his text *The Web of Life* as "the body of concepts, and perceptions shared by a community that form a particular vision of reality, serves as the basis upon which the community organizes itself, and is used by that community to define problems, as well as find solutions" (p. 5). Each culture has its own paradigm used to interpret experiences and frame the stories it tells. Furthermore, each generation believes its perspective is slightly more privileged than those preceding them. Nonetheless, as Malcolm Gladwell (2000) states, paradigms may shift when there is a critical mass or "tipping point" consensus to change the paradigm. Thereafter, the paradigm takes on a new meaning and has more explanatory power than the old. The evolving paradigm creates a new framework for interpreting experience that influences and transcends the previous one. Therefore, the society possesses a new way of perceiving themselves. This new "knowing" manifests itself in their ethics, morals, values, politics, art, music, literature, religion, science, education, and, in fact, just about every aspect of their culture.

EDUCATION IS IN A MUDDLE

Such is the case for the paradigm of today's American education. The story we tell harks back to the nineteenth century when children were trained with skills that prepared them for an adult life working in the factories of the industrial era. The nineteenth-century "clockwork" paradigm provided further structure to education. The metaphor of the "factory" became the working definition of how to instruct children. Children's minds were viewed as "commodities" produced by moving through an "assembly-line" of disciplines (e.g., mathematics, science, English, history) in specific "clockwork" schedules using the agrarian calendar so some children could work in their parents' farms.

This "mechanistic" framework is a far cry from the "organic" living system discussed earlier in chapter 2. Knowledge was viewed as the main product that students were taught to *acquire.* Learning was a *means to an end* rather than an *end itself.* However, the problem is that while time changed the world, educational systems did not keep pace with it. If you traveled back to the mid-nineteenth century, you'd find a teacher standing in front of the room lecturing thirty students in rows of desks. With the exception of technology, this is pretty much the way classroom teaching is today. *Educating from a nineteenth-century industrial age paradigm no longer satisfies the needs of learners living in the twenty-first-century digital age.*

Twenty-first-century school frameworks have been designed and proposed in various ways. Nonetheless, they all discuss how to integrate new technology, new pedagogies, interdisciplinary curricula, open learning spaces, and reformed teacher training, to name a few (Fielding, 2001; Jackson & Davis, 2000; MacDonald & Hursh, 2006; Yates, 2007). A core component of all twenty-first-century frameworks is the need to develop and adopt a "whole-student" approach. Moreover, this approach addresses learners' social, emotional, moral, and intellectual development (Cain & Carnellor, 2008; McCombs, 2004; Noddings, 1995; Palmer, 2003).

The National Scientific Council on the Developing Child (2006, p. 7) states:

> If we really want to build a strong platform for healthy development and effective learning . . . then we must pay as much attention to children's emotional well-being and social capacities as we do to their cognitive abilities and academic skills. (p. 7)

THE LEARNING COMPACT RENEWED: WHOLE CHILD FOR THE WHOLE WORLD

The Association for Supervision and Curriculum Development (ASCD) has for the past thirteen years emphasized the need for a change in American education that supports all aspects of students' lives. The following is a quotation from ASCD's Commission on the Whole Child as cited in *The Learning Compact Renewed: Whole Child for the Whole World* (2017). It states the consequences of not teaching the whole child:

> If we concentrate solely on academics and on narrowly measured academic achievement, we fail to educate the whole child. We shortchange our young people and limit their future if we do not create places of learning that encourage and celebrate every aspect of each student's capacity for learning. We can do more, and we can do better. (p. 8)

ASCD advocated at the federal level by proposing the Whole Child Resolution to Congress in 2010. This resolution was subsequently passed in 2014. The next year ASCD successfully advocated for increased accountability: "Beyond math and reading, use multiple measures and include nonacademic factors (e.g. school climate, school safety, parent engagement)" (ASCD, 2017 p. 11) vis-à-vis the Elementary and Secondary Education Act. With that report, ASCD launched a new project—the Whole Child Initiative—to redefine learning in the twenty-first century.

The thrust of their new initiative set out to open up a dialogue among educators to take a fresh look at fostering the long-term success of learners. (ASCD, 2017). Linda Darling-Hammond, as cited in *The Learning Compact Renewed*, eloquently defined the Whole-Child approach:

> A whole child approach seeks to address the distinctive strengths, needs, and interests of students as they engage in learning. . . . All aspects of children's being are supported in an effort to ensure that learning happens in deep, meaningful, and lasting ways. (p. 14)

In 2015, on the heels of the adoption of the Whole Child Resolution, the Obama administration passed the Every Student Succeeds Act (ESSA), which provided states with more flexibility regarding how best to assess students. ASCD's Whole-Child approach comes at a time when the world in which today's children live has changed in unprecedented ways. They now live in a global society that is changing faster than at any other time in history.

Today's children are exposed to high levels of uncertainty and unpredictability in most facets of their lives. Industrialization has fanned the fires of a fossil fuel–based culture to give rise to air pollution that has spawned unprecedented climate changes resulting in altering global biomes. Glaciers are melting at an unprecedented rate while tropical storms are intensifying and rainforests are disappearing, causing animal and plant species to become extinct in one's lifetime.

We have become dependent upon technology in almost every aspect of how we conduct ourselves daily. Moreover, our appetite for technology is changing the way we learn and share information. Today's children are living in the digital age. This revolution in technology will result in today's children likely having several careers in their lifetimes. The industrial age skills that supported life and work in the twentieth century are no longer sufficient to prepare citizens to thrive in the twenty-first century.

Therefore what is needed now, more than during the previous century, is a new framework for learning and schooling. ASCD's Whole-Child approach is an ethos to educate the whole child in promoting:

- physical and emotional health;
- well-being and safety;
- opportunities to actively participate in curricular, extracurricular, and community activities;
- highly qualified, dedicated, and caring educators who offer engaging and meaningful learning activities and rigorous curricula; and
- college and career success. (ASCD, 2017)

The ASCD report further maintains that today's schools should focus on the four Cs—collaboration, creativity, communication, and critical thinking. (ASCD, 2017, p. 40)

In 2015, Education Reimagined, an esteemed group composed of twenty-eight educators, scholars, businesspeople, parents, and advocates, came together to discuss and ultimately create a new vision for education in a document called "A Transformational Vision for Education in the United States." Their mission took form on the basis of the inability of the current educational system to meet the demands and needs of today's youngsters: "Simply put the current system was designed in a different era and structured for a different society. . . . In order to envision something new, we engaged in a challenging, dialogic process to reimagine learning" (pp. 2–3). The guiding purpose they built upon was "to enable all children to fulfill their full potential as empowered individuals, constructive members of their communities, productive participants in the economy and engaged citizens of the US and the world" (p. 3).

The cadre of dedicated professionals were committed to transforming education in order to empower all students to reach their full potential. Their twenty-first-century framework emerged from the fact that the nineteenth-century factory model no longer adequately prepares our youth for a rapidly changing global society that demands a different set of right-brain skills. Daniel Pink (2005) refers to these as "high touch" (i.e., capacity to get along with others) and "high concept" skills (i.e., envisioning the big picture).

Collectively the authors of the *Learning Compact* (2015) believe "that the current system's one-to-many approach to teaching, standardized curriculum, age-based cohorts, and classroom-contained instruction are all limitations on our children's opportunities to learn and thrive in this changing world" (p. 4). Their proposal calls for a shift in the way children learn. This is a shift from a "school-centered" (i.e., *school-centric*) to a "Whole-Child" (i.e., *student-centric*) approach whereby learning is viewed as a lifelong process. This is a shift from the industrial age's *school-centric* approach designed to efficiently deliver discipline-based curricula in a standardized way. The networked age *student-centric* approach is designed to adapt education to the needs of each learner to foster achieving their highest potential. This new approach is characterized by:

- personalizing learning;
- creating learning experiences that foster learners' ability to create knowledge, skills, and habits of mind; and
- learners situated in a network of supportive relationships with adults who encourage self-directed paths to learning and problem solving.

One of the most important factors of their new student-centric framework is "tearing" down the walls of classrooms to create "open" classrooms. Open classrooms are the consequence of learners using community and Internet resources to learn and problem solve. This fosters a more personalized, technologically based learning process for learners to find and learn what they need to know. Of course, this doesn't eliminate the teacher. Rather the role of the teacher is reframed to that of a coach, guide, or facilitator who, nonetheless, evaluates students' learning with competency-based assessments.

THE WHOLE-CHILD LEARNER PARADIGM

The *Learning Compact* and Education Reimagined initiatives envisioned *transforming* rather than merely *reforming* American education. Their visions to transform education are educationally sound frameworks for learning and thinking aimed at all American students. Nonetheless, getting the leadership at the national, state, and local levels to buy into adopting it is another challenge. So the next question becomes how to bring about any change, especially a large and sweeping shift in perspective that is being envisioned here.

Both of these Whole-Child approaches offer a student-centric approach to teaching and learning. However, while they emphasize the importance of developing a Whole-Child framework, they do not provide a new "narrative" that provides educators and especially policy-makers with a concise, well-articulated, and jargon-free "storyline." This new narrative defines the learning process as the result of interactions between learners and their physical and social environment.

A Whole-Child narrative needs to explicitly provide a comprehensive discussion of how to foster a meaningful approach to learning and relating to others. Moreover, it needs to discuss the specific cognitive (i.e., thinking skills), social (i.e., interpersonal skills), and emotional (i.e., well-being) needs of students. More importantly, it outlines how to effectively address and meet them. Furthermore, to be effective, a Whole-Child narrative needs to clearly convey that these needs demand the adoption and concerted efforts of the *entire school system*.

Therefore, what follows is an integrated Whole-Child framework predicated on illustrating the dynamic interdependencies of the influences affecting the learning process. Each learner has outside influences that affect the learning process, as well as ways of demonstrating learning. Moreover, learners can demonstrate learning from a personal or social perspective.

1. The *educator-based influences* consist of the *educational techniques/ strategies and approaches employed to teach students* aspects of the learning environment. Although not exclusively, these include:

   - right/left brain thinking skills;
   - deep processing skills;
   - social and emotional skills and emotional intelligence;
   - interdisciplinary curricula;
   - constructivist pedagogies;
   - collaborative grouping; and
   - CBL, PBL, and PBE.

2. *District-based influences* consist of the *objective* aspects of the learning environment. These include:

   - classroom structure (arrangement of student workspaces);
   - access to technology;

- school grading and behavioral standards;
- national and discipline-based curricular standards;
- mission and vision statements; and
- board of education policy statements.

3. *Personal demonstrations* of expressing a growth mindset take the form of:

   - demonstrating competency in using deep processing thinking skills;
   - taking a meaningful approach to learning;
   - demonstrating conceptual understanding;
   - using the imagination to think "outside the box";
   - demonstrating insight in solving problems;
   - demonstrating creativity;
   - developing problem-solving skills; and
   - displaying resilience and perseverance when provided with challenging tasks.

4. *Interpersonal demonstrations* of learning are demonstrative ways of expressing subjective or qualitative aspects of the learning process. These qualities include:

   - empathy;
   - compassion;
   - social-emotional learning skills;
   - embracing diversity;
   - displaying well-being; and
   - demonstrating emotional intelligence.

From an educational perspective, while each of the influences/ways of demonstrating learning is unique and different, none is independent of any other. Therefore, as the arrows in figure 3.1 demonstrate, the school- and educator-based influences not only affect each other but also impact the personal and interpersonal ways learners express learning.

Through the interdependent relationships among all influences and learning demonstrations, the Whole-Child educator can foster the emergence of the competent and Whole-Child learner. This integrated approach helps educators understand how students develop *rationally, aesthetically, socially, and emotionally* in becoming more integrated individuals. The Whole-Child learner paradigm provides insight to understanding how *being mindful of both educator-based and district-based influences affects personal and interpersonal demonstrations of learning*. Toward this end, the learner-centered

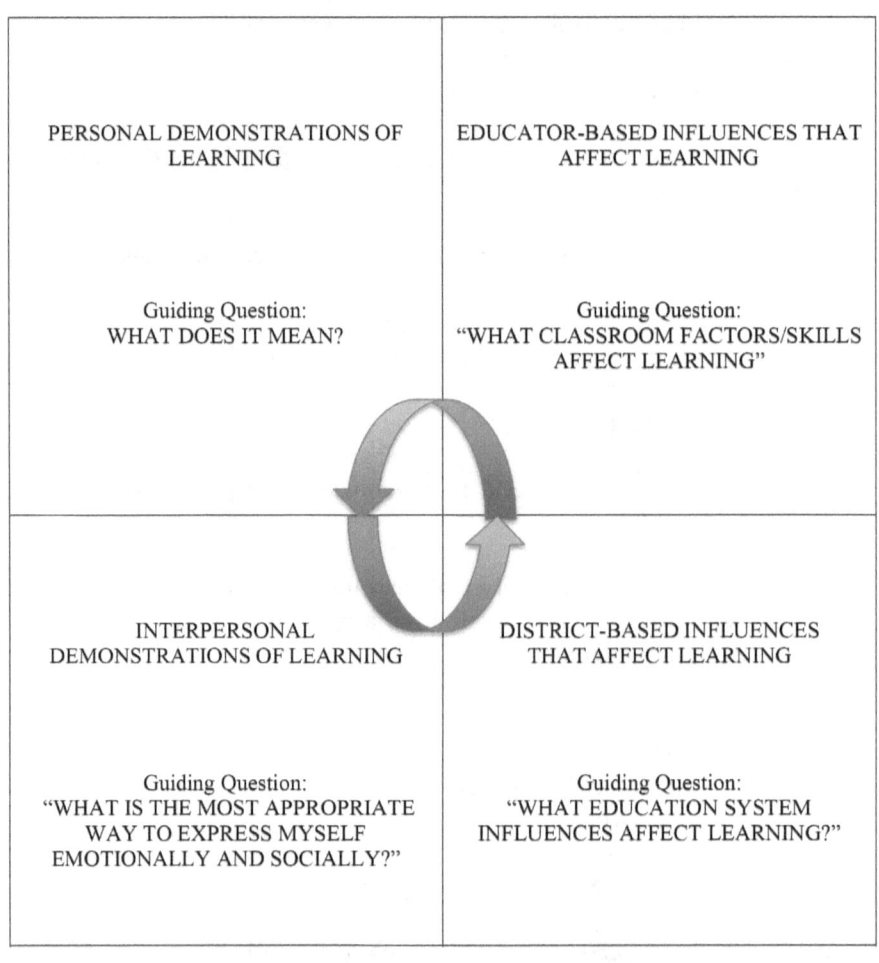

Figure 3.1. The Interdependent Facets of the Whole-Child Paradigm. *Author created*

educator needs to employ teaching strategies and pedagogies that foster the development of the whole child.

Students' motivation to learn derives from the drive to create meaning within the context of the Whole-Child paradigm as a whole and competent individual. Furthermore, as social constructivist psychologists (e.g., Bruner, 1990) have noted, the learner is *situated within* as well as *distributed throughout* his or her physical and social environment. As a consequence, educators need to appreciate how their culture defines the learner. Students manifest themselves in the form of an ever-changing personal narrative.

Moreover, students provided with a nurturing education milieu will grow and flourish toward becoming a contributing member of society.

Figure 3.1 illustrates the Whole-Child paradigm. The basis of this paradigm lies in the fact that each quadrant is interrelated and codependent upon all the others. For instance, if the goal is to foster social and emotional learning, the Whole-Child *educator* needs to integrate social and emotional learning strategies into their classroom lessons. However, this alone will not suffice in meeting this goal.

The *school- and district-based* policies must embrace fostering social and emotional learning as a high priority in the school and district. Therefore, the staff is provided with extensive professional development training in ways to integrate and foster social and emotional learning skills in their classroom teaching.

Moreover, learners must be able to demonstrate *interpersonal* skills that display social and emotional learning. This is an ongoing cycle whereby the *educator* becomes aware of the extent to which learners display social and emotional learning and adapt their lessons accordingly. Toward this end, fostering social and emotional skills needs to be fully integrated into the classroom teaching rather than as a stand-alone lesson. Therefore, social and emotional learning becomes a central feature of the school and educator's educational intention.

If the goal is to foster a *meaningful approach to learning*, then the *district-based* policies and mission must encourage *educators* to adopt constructivist pedagogies, as well as foster a growth mindset. Toward this end, educators will create lessons that foster tenacity, resilience, and grit. A growth mindset fosters deep understanding. Thus, the district-based policies and mission provide an educational framework for *educators* to create dynamic lessons that foster a growth mindset.

To transform education requires the integration of both *district-based* policies and specific *educator-based* strategies and pedagogies. The extent to which these are successful is assessed by *personal* demonstrations of meaningful learning, growth mindset, and competency in using deep processing thinking skills. In both of the above examples, we see that either *personal* or *interpersonal* demonstrations of learning do not occur in a vacuum. Rather they are codependent upon both *educator-based* and *district-based* influences.

Thus this dynamic framework is predicated upon a holistic and systemic approach to addressing the cognitive, social, and emotional needs of the *whole child*. This is in contrast to the current model where *personal* and *interpersonal* learning is left to the *educator*. Thus, in many cases, teachers are left to their own devices to decide the extent to which they foster social and emotional skills (or not) as well as a growth mindset. A systemic transformation would result in teachers being supported and championed by the entire educational system.

SUMMARY

Using this framework, the Whole-Child educator can mindfully approach teaching by fulfilling the needs of the *whole* student. The Whole-Child educator views learning as a process. Therefore, they employ constructivist pedagogies designed to engage students with dynamic lessons. Learners have specific roles and responsibilities to actively participate in taking a meaningful approach to their studies. Teachers serve as facilitators to create learning opportunities for their students to demonstrate competency in developing understanding.

Moreover, the school system's mission and vision statements shape these roles and responsibilities. What is equally important for the Whole-Child educator is to foster the development of social and emotional learning competencies. *It is only by viewing the four quadrants of the Whole-Child learner as interdependent aspects of learners* that we are able to understand how to optimize learning.

II

The District-Based Influences That Affect Learning and Thinking

*What Are the Metaphors and Values for the
Twenty-First-Century Whole-Child Education Story?*

Chapter Four

Creating a New Story of Learning and Thinking

If we teach today's students as we taught yesterday's, we rob them of tomorrow.—John Dewey

LEARNING AS PRODUCT OR PROCESS?

As previously discussed, Western society is in the midst of a revolutionary shift transforming scientific and social paradigms alike. This new process-based vision has changed the educational metaphor from one of noun-based *learning as product* to that of the verb-based *learning as process*. Proponents of this new framework assume that the transformation of information into understanding can only be gained through an integrated and holistic approach.

This holistic approach fosters a paradigm that emphasizes unity, connectedness, purpose, and meaning. The Whole-Child paradigm was introduced in the last chapter. In order to make the holistic nature of this framework more readily accessible to educators, what is needed is a new narrative. Therefore the details of a new story and metaphors are the focus of this chapter.

The role and responsibility of the school superintendent, central office staff, and building administrators is to serve as the district's chief education leaders. This translates into providing the district with a sound educational framework with which to guide teachers in performing their roles. Their mission and vision statements must provide a clear, coherent, and concise *narrative* to guide the district's educators in their pursuit of education excellence.

The central message of this book is that this narrative needs to provide the district with a "storyline" that creates an educational culture grounded in a Whole-Child approach to teaching and learning. Moreover, it is the responsibility of the board of education to embrace and support this vision especially with respect to working with the town government officials to secure sufficient funding to support the implementation of this vision.

A WHOLE-CHILD EDUCATIONAL FRAMEWORK

Overly simplistic ways of knowing view knowledge as "private" and thus discount the participatory interplay between learners and their culture. Whole-Child ways of knowing consider "freedom" of the individual to develop a sense of *relationship and belonging*. Whole-Child approaches view learners as belonging to and evolving within an interconnected world that can readily be experienced firsthand through insight, intuition, and mindfulness practices.

Compassionately reaching out to others and engaging the whole self in the cultivation of relationships inherently fosters a sense of belonging. Belonging, in this sense, is most likely to evolve in an environment that stresses caring, nurturing, and the cultivation of relationships. Hence, the Whole-Child educational philosophy advocates and promotes learning through fostering *mutuality, dialogue, and responsibility* as the essential complements of belongingness.

In this book, I argue that policy makers need to adopt a Whole-Child perspective, which presumes all learners' needs are intrinsically *interrelated*. Moreover, it suggests that meaning is *contextual*. Thus, nothing of and by itself has any absolute or inherent *meaning*. Meaning is vital to understanding and therefore learning. A Whole-Child educational framework is therefore predicated upon the following six thematic elements.

1. *Transcend the current American mindset.* The current mindset promotes and sustains the static and impersonal world of the nineteenth-century framework. We need to adopt a new paradigm driven to promote, maintain, and generate a dynamic and meaningful approach to learning.
2. *Tear down the artificial barriers to knowing* we have come to refer to as "disciplines." This entails refocusing our attention to embrace an interdisciplinary approach to learning.
3. *Redefine the role of "learner" and "teacher"* as cocreators in the learning process.
4. *Renew what it means to be a "teacher"* whose role is to "draw out" natural inclinations and abilities, rather than "pour in" information.

This new role of facilitator and coach doesn't preclude teaching content. Rather their role is to raise students' awareness that learning is a consequence of actively processing *information* into *knowledge* and meaningfully transforming it into *understanding*.

5. *Promote meaningful and alternative approaches to learning and thinking.* These approaches encourage use of learning strategies that promote use of higher-order thinking skills.
6. *Explore dimensions of human experience* other than the logical and linguistic ways of knowing. Learner-centered teaching methods include Howard Gardner's multiple intelligences, as well as Daniel Pink's "right-brain" skills. Pink (2005) concludes educators need to foster the development of a new generation of creators who—as "artists, inventors, designers, storytellers, caregivers, consolers, big picture thinkers—will now reap society's richest rewards and share its greatest joys" (p. 3). Additionally, in *The Arts and the Creation of Mind*, Eisner (2002) presents strong arguments for the inclusion of aesthetics as a core element of the school curriculum for all children. Since the 1960s, Eisner has steadily promoted arts education to enrich connections between thinking and learning in the arts with other disciplines.

AN AUTHENTIC CURRICULUM

The art of Whole-Child educational practice involves responding *authentically* to the needs of children, curriculum, and the culture without rigidly adhering to a specific methodology. Characteristics such as *authenticity, empathy, mindfulness, and sensitivity* are qualities one might find in educators operating within a holistic framework. This type of learning seeks to promote what David Sobel (2004) and his colleagues at Antioch New England Graduate School call an "authentic curriculum." This term goes by others such as *integrated curriculum, developmentally appropriate curriculum*, and *thematic curriculum*.

Essentially the authentic curriculum is built upon recognizing and supporting Martin Buber's "I-Thou" whereby the relationship between the child, teacher, and the curriculum are interdependent. The key word here is "relationship." Teaching from this perspective means being mindful to the myriad learning opportunities that typically occur during the day. Fostering these relationships emerges by providing learning opportunities for students to recognize and appreciate learning as a meaning-making process.

As a consequence of learning in this manner, the student begins to view the curriculum as alive with potential opportunities to learn, grow, and construct meaning. Taking time to momentarily follow the students' interests promotes a stronger sense of students' self-worth and confidence.

To effectively implement any new whole-school initiative requires a deep examination of the district's learning and thinking "culture." This culture defines the roles that students, parents, educators, and administrators play in the learning process. In his book *Creating Cultures of Thinking*, Ron Ritchhart (2015) makes and supports a strong argument that before we can reform, let alone transform, our schools, we need to come to an agreement as to:

- *why* do we educate in the first place and
- *what* does a "quality" education mean?

Before we go any further, we need to address each of these questions to more fully understand why America needs to create a new narrative from which to transform education. Ritchhart suggests this new narrative needs to change the way we not only view education but also the way in which we assess it. Arts advocate Elliott Eisner (2002) said: "As long as schools treat test scores as the major proxies for student achievment and educational quality we will have a hard time refocusing our attention on what really matters" (p. 9).

WHY DO WE EDUCATE IN THE FIRST PLACE?

In a *New York Times Magazine* essay, "How to Remake Education," education historian and vocal advocate Diane Ravitch (2009) asked:

> Why do we educate? We educate because we want citizens who are capable of taking responsibility for their lives and for our democracy. We want citizens who understand how their government works, who are knowledgeable about the history of their nation and other nations. We need citizens who are thoroughly educated in science. We need people who can communicate in other languages. We must ensure that every young person has the chance to engage in the arts. (p. 33)

Education should not only be for our youth but rather a lifelong process whereby we continually learn the skills requisite to not only survive but also thrive in an ever-changing world. Not only do we educate to prepare students for college and or career success but also to prepare them for life. This is especially true for today's youth, who will likely have several careers in their lifetimes. This explosion in new career choices is due to the unprecedented growth in new technologies and services, most of which have yet to emerge.

Being educated is a prerequisite to making a good living and realizing a productive life. Thus, the father of pragmatism, Charles Sanders Pierce, believed that everything, especially thought, was in dynamic process rather than in a static form of being. Pierce's pragmatism essentially asked the question: "What can it do?" (Fabriches, 2019). Therefore, he would say education serves a pragmatic purpose to make our ideas clear and bring about specific outcomes, which today are primarily economic in nature.

Moreover, being educated fosters the ability to communicate both orally and in written form, think critically, and problem solve, all of which are essential skills of living in today's world. In *The Flat World and Education: How America's Commitment to Equity Will Determine Our Future* (2010), Linda Darling-Hammond states that the purpose of education is to teach students "to read and write effectively, reason mathematically, inquire scientifically, play music, draw and paint, and understand and analyze history, geography, and social phenomena in the world around them" (p. 297). In *Democracy and Education*, Dewey (1916) built upon the idea central to his philosophy of education: "If democracy has a moral and ideal meaning, it is that a social return be demanded from all and that opportunity for development of distinctive capacities be afforded all" (p. 129).

In 2018, the Organisation for Economic Co-operation and Development published a position paper called *The Future of Education and Skills*. This paper offered the following reasons why the purpose of education should not exclusively be for the purpose of preparing students for career success.

> In the face of an increasingly volatile, uncertain, complex and ambiguous world, education can make the difference as to whether people embrace the challenges they are confronted with or whether they are defeated by them. And in an era characterized by a new explosion of scientific knowledge and a growing array of complex societal problems, it is appropriate that curricula should continue to evolve, perhaps in radical ways. (p. 3)

Thus, with John Dewey's pragmatism came a new goal of education—children possess unique talents that should be nurtured. Moreover, Dewey's pragmatism focused on socializing and developing informed citizens who are socially conscious and possess a civic responsibility to come to the aid of their community. In *The School and Society* (1899), Dewey advocated for a "Copernican" revolution in education whereby "the child becomes the sun around which the appliances of education revolve; he is the center about which they are organized" (p. 23). Therefore, to Dewey, being educated ensures freethinking citizens whereby democracy becomes a way of life. This enables informed citizens to feel empowered to voice their opinion in the voting booth. Dewey's pragmatism is becoming more relevant in today's global community where our actions and politics impact countries outside our borders. Thus, today's education has the challenge of developing children's personhood and citizenship.

WHAT DOES A "QUALITY" EDUCATION MEAN?

In his classic *Zen and the Art of Motorcycle Maintenance* (1980) and its sequel, *Lila* (1992), Robert Pirsig reveals a deep and more philosophical treatise on morals that we'll see is readily relevant to transforming education. He sees "quality" as ultimately responsible for creating the patterns of the universe and therefore matter and mind. He proposes a "metaphysics of quality" that can be used to reunite the disparate fields of art, religion, and science into a new and more holistic framework. He takes quality to be the primary reality and splits it into two dimensions: *static and dynamic*.

Reality as perceived by Pirsig consists of four static patterns of value (inorganic, biological, social, and intellectual). Each of these evolve and exist in response to one another through "dynamic quality." While a human life requires static patterns (e.g., food, genetically controlled metabolic patterns, social relationships, and learning), one cannot grow and develop as a unique individual without responding to dynamic patterns of quality. Pirsig states that humans are collections of value patterns.

Moreover, these may grow and evolve to varying extents, due to their free ability to respond to or ignore new creative dynamic quality. According to Pirsig, what's good in life isn't defined by any static pattern—biological, social, or intellectual. Rather, what's good is *freedom* from the constraints of any static pattern and the ability to respond creatively and adapt to one's situation.

> The Metaphysics of Quality resolves the relationship between intellect and society, subject and object, mind and matter, by embedding all of them in a larger system of understanding. Objects are inorganic and biological values; subjects are social and intellectual values. They have a matter-of-fact evolutionary relationship. That evolutionary relationship is also a moral one. (Pirsig, 1992, p. 344)

While Pirsig's books are fictional and entertaining, they offer insight into how "quality" should frame teaching and learning in the classroom. The traditional educational design is predicated on the expectations and values of the *static* industrial age. The industrial age narrative viewed schooling as preparatory to entering the workforce. On the other hand, the Whole-Child narrative is based on the *dynamic* digital age whereby growth, creativity, imagination, and innovation are fostered for an evolving culture.

WHAT ARE THE METAPHORS OF THE TWENTIETH-CENTURY EDUCATIONAL STORY?

Creating a new culture of learning and thinking requires adopting new metaphors and values. The meaning of "value" is the intrinic worth of something. A culture's paradigm defines the beliefs that establish the values, which subsequently determine behaviors. Therefore, with a change in the paradigm come changes in beliefs, values, and behaviors. The values a society embraces have much to say about the nature of what they believe is important. Values serve as our moral compass to keep us on our chosen course. Our core values are the standards with which we make decisions and choices every day.

The metaphors that characterize a society are a reflection of the values they embrace and live by. Therefore, if values change, the metaphors representing them also change. A systemic change in education requires a cultural change in the philosophical perspectives for the role of teacher and student. What follows are the major and derivative metaphors defining the values for both the twentieth- and twenty-first-century cultures of education.

The major metaphor lying at the heart of the twentieth-century story is *learning as a product* whereas the major metaphor underlying the twenty-first-century story is *learning as a process*. *The dilemma of the Whole-Child educator is trying to educate from a learner-centered value system in a culture predominated by one that espouses a teacher-centered educational approach.* What follows is a comparison of the metaphors characteristic of the twentieth- and twenty-first-century educational approaches.

ORIENTATIONS ON CLASSROOM THINKING AND LEARNING

Twentieth-Century Story

Major Metaphor: Learning as PRODUCT
  Derivative Metaphors:

- Principals are *chief managerial officers.*
- *Teacher evaluations* take into consideration the *time on task* students work on their assignments.
- Administrators use *value-added measures to assess* the contribution of *a teacher* to their students' standardized test scores.
- Knowledge is a product produced by requiring *high-quality control.*
- Educators are trained in how to *manage* classrooms and *discipline* students.
- Educators are held responsible for *students' performance.*
- Learning is construed as merchandizable *"goods" or a product.*

- Educators are taught how to *work efficiently*.
- Classrooms are places where laborers (students) *work*.
- Knowledge, assessed by test scores and grades, is the end-product of learning.

Twenty-First-Century Story

Major Metaphor: Learning as PROCESS
  Derivative Metaphors:

- Principals are *educational leaders*.
- Educators look for strategies that *promote meaningful approaches to learning* and how to engage learners.
- Knowledge is the basis on which *understanding is developed*.
- Educators are trained in ways to *promote learning and thinking*.
- Learners are *coparticipants* in the learning process.
- Learning is construed as *personal growth*.
- Students are learners who are taught how to use *cognitive and metacognitive learning strategies*.
- Classrooms are *playscapes*.
- Learning is an *end in itself*.

WHAT IS THE TWENTIETH-CENTURY-STORY BEING "TOLD" IN MOST AMERICAN CLASSROOMS?

In a typical twentieth-century teacher-centered classroom, students sat in neat rows and were taught how to work independently in separate disciplines. However, declining standardized test scores were interpreted to be the result of a failing education system. As discussed in chapter 1, nationally inspired education reform efforts from No Child Left Behind (NCLB) and to the Every Student Succeeds Act (ESSA)—together with the Common Core State Standards (CCSS)—are leading American schools down the wrong path.

Collectively these reform efforts have been *regressive, repressive, and, in some cases, oppressive*. Moreover, these reform initiatives have turned a deaf ear to educators who, as highly educated professionals, are trained to know how best to develop young minds. The tragic irony is that these reform efforts are based on a nineteenth-century mindset that is intended to prepare students for success in the twenty-first century. However, to paraphrase Einstein, we can't solve problems by using the same kind of thinking we used when we created them.

The twentieth-century story, like the recent reform efforts, was designed to systematize, standardize, and align the learning process using a "factory" model of "one size fits all." This mindset is flawed in many ways. First of all, it assumes that the learning process can be distilled to a few objective and quantitative measures. Moreover, these measures exclude those due to socioeconomic inequities, which cannot be remedied from within the educational system. Nonetheless, what matters most to fostering the learning process are intangibles that are not easily quantified.

Einstein stated it more eloquently: "Not everything that can be counted counts, and not everything that counts can be counted." Secondly, using the CCSS to assess student learning is a misguided approach. Many of the standards of the CCSS are not supported by empirical studies, which invalidate their use as substantive to measuring the skill and knowledge base proficiency requisite to be deemed "educated." Thirdly, while some standards of the CCSS are welcomed, mandating the use of all the CCSS undermines the development of the imagination, creativity, and innovation that made this nation a leading world power.

Lastly, linking student performance to standardized assessments evaluating educators is not only unsound but also counterproductive to improving education in the first place. The major flaw inherent to the "current story" is that it assumes that excellence in teaching and learning can be *objectively* measured.

The following points summarize the educational ethos of the twentieth-century story:

- teachers "pour" facts into students;
- teachers are driven to "cover" the curriculum;
- teachers are the "sage on the stage";
- teaching is a "science";
- teachers use instructionist pedagogies;
- learning is textbook driven;
- assignments are "time-based";
- learning is "passive" and occurs in "isolation";
- teacher-focused;
- teachers are authorities;
- fragmented curriculum;
- evaluation is by teacher-created summative assessments; and
- low expectations.

WHAT IS THE TWENTY-FIRST-CENTURY STORY WE WANT TO "TELL" IN AMERICAN CLASSROOMS?

If we as a society are going to survive, we need to embrace the emerging education paradigm that views the mind, learning, and thinking in a more holistic and integrated framework. What is needed is a paradigm shift in what this country's leaders recognize as the skill set of thinking and learning processes indispensable for success in the twenty-first century.

Harvard educator Ron Ritchhart (2015) refers to the *purpose and promise* of education as that which provides the skills and competencies to flourish in society. Tony Wagner, Daniel Pink, Howard Gardner, Elliot Eisner, and others have defined the skills and competencies needed to succeed in the twenty-first century. The cognitive skills, habits of mind, and learning dispositions will be further discussed in chapter 7.

Much to the dismay of corporate and political reformers is the fact that several of these skills and dispositions are difficult, if not impossible, to objectively assess with a standardized test. These skills build upon and transcend Bloom's revised taxonomy. The fear among these experts is that if we place too much emphasis on "mastering" knowledge without *also* developing these types of skills and dispositions, then we are not "walking the talk."

A school's mission involves *more* than mere mastery of curricular content. Rather it involves encouraging a lifetime love of learning to develop independent and creative problem solvers. Toward this end, we need to rely less on high-stakes testing. In their place, we need to develop ways to improve learning. Therefore, I contend that policy makers need to include professional educators in the dialogue.

Government officials and corporate leaders may have the best of intentions in attempting to reform American education. However, authentic educational change can only arise from professional educators. Educators possess the expertise, dedication, and passion that enable them to meet the needs and challenges in educating children for the twenty-first century. The Whole-Child educator has a vested interest in education that enhances the way children are prepared for life in the twenty-first century. Moreover, they understand the strategies and practices that foster students adopting more meaningful approaches to learning and thinking. The outcome of this challenge is to provide educators with a renewed vision of what a quality education looks like.

SUMMARY

Therefore, the Whole-Child paradigm explains to educators why the twentieth-century story no longer serves to prepare learners for success in the twenty-first century. Embracing the Whole-Child paradigm changes the metaphor from *learning as a "product"* to *learning as a "process."* The difference is that the *former views learning as the means to an end* whereas the *latter views learning as an end in and of itself.*

As linguists Edward Sapir and Benjamin Whorf suggested, there is a significant relationship between the language people use and how they think, perceive, and define causal relationships. Viewing learning as a means rather than an end limits it to being perceived as an end-product rather than a process to create understanding in and of itself.

Whole-Child educators serve as facilitators that prompt students to adopt a meaningful approach to learning. Thus, the focus is on learning, which typically occurs in collaborative groups. Their curriculum is interdisciplinary and relevant to students' interests and experience. Efforts are made to ensure what students learn is derived from and/or applicable to real-life situations.

III

The Educator-Based Influences That Affect Learning and Thinking

How Can a Whole-Child Approach to Teaching Foster Development of the Skills Requisite to Thrive in the Twenty-First Century?

Chapter Five

What Are the Teaching Practices of the Teacher-Centered and Learner-Centered Approaches to Teaching?

> *What we want is to see the child in pursuit of knowledge, and not knowledge in pursuit of the child.*—George Bernard Shaw

As we discussed in the last chapter, there are two predominant teaching approaches that educators adopt. The teacher-centered approach best characterizes the teaching style used in the twentieth century and the emerging learner-centered one the teaching style used in the twenty-first century. What follows is an overview of each teaching style for each of the following categories:

- the perception of their role as an educator,
- the purpose of teaching,
- approach to learning,
- risk-taking, and
- what they consider when creating lessons.

TWENTIETH-CENTURY CLASSROOM TEACHING PRACTICES: LEARNING AS PRODUCT

Teacher-Centered

Teachers perceive the need to:

- view themselves as instructors who deliver knowledge as a *"commodity"* whose production requires high quality control;
- *dominate "talk" time* so as "cover" the lesson for the day;
- *rarely demonstrate their* curiosity, passion, and interest in students;
- *rarely display open-mindedness* and willingness to consider alternative perspectives;
- *seldom take notice and acknowledge* the thinking occurring in the classroom;
- treat learners as isolated *members* of a class;
- demonstrate *thinking is not* a "school as usual practice";
- ensure all students respect each other's possessions;
- *ideas and students may be challenged*;
- ensure that visitors are easily able to discern what the classroom educator cares about and values with *respect to knowledge*;
- show a genuine curiosity and interest in learners' *test results*;
- listen in on groups to ensure all are on the *"right track"* making them act dependently on teacher expectations;
- provide *little time for students to extend, elaborate, or develop ideas* of others in order to "cover the curriculum";
- arrange classroom desks to ensure *teachers are the constant focus of attention*; and
- perceive classrooms as *workplaces* within which students work to learn the details of the curriculum.

Teachers demonstrate the purpose of teaching by:

- believing that the purpose of school is to *foster knowledge acqusition*;
- perceiving *thinking as an "add-on"* to the lesson;
- providing *insufficient class-time for learners to process concepts* in order to "cover" the lesson for the day;
- focusing students' attention on numerous curricular details, names, dates, and so forth that *require memorization* rather than creating meaningful connections of curriculum to world;
- *rarely, if ever, providing opportunities* for learners *to reflect* on how their thinking has changed over time;
- using thinking routines effectively to deepen students' *acquisition of knowledge*;
- *using routines and structures to help students organize their learning space* to do what they do in class;
- encouraging use of *surface learning strategies*; and
- using quantitative measures to gauge students' level of knowledge.

Teachers foster a rote approach to learning by:

- providing students with learning opportunities to *demonstrate competency* of what they have learned;
- drawing upon effective routines and structures to help students organize their knowledge acquisition ing using *lower-order thinking skills*;
- developing comptency to use mostly "lower" (*rote thinking*) skills on Bloom's taxonomy (e.g., remember, recall, list, describe);
- demonstrating an authentic interest in and fostering students *knowledge acquisition*;
- fostering development of a *fixed mindset*;
- typically making time for student contributions *if he/she has "covered" the lesson* for the day;
- *not requiring students to model thought processes* by providing evidence for their thinking;
- pushing students to *get the right answer*; and
- *rarely demonstrating* their curiosity, passion, and interest in students.

Teachers discourage risk-taking by:

- impressing upon students that *mistakes are not acceptable* and are to be avoided;
- emphasizing that it's *not good to take learning risks* because you might make a mistake;
- *rarely taking learning risks* and not demonstrating themselves as reflective learners; and
- providing learners with *ability attributions* for success or failure.

Teachers create lessons that:

- *rarely provide students with opportunities* to direct their own learning to *become independent learners*;
- *rarely*, if at all, ensure rich *thinking opportunities*;
- rarely provide the time for students to *extend, elaborate, or develop ideas of others*;
- *foster learners' competency in using skills that enhance the acquisition of knowledge*;
- foster students to become dependent on their teachers to ascertain their *level of performance*;
- promote *teacher-dependent* learners;
- rarely provide group activities whereby students exchange ideas as they *work collaboratively* on assignments; and
- provide students with *structured learning assignments* with specified outcomes.

Twentieth-Century Educator Practices

The twentieth-century teacher-centered story is reflective of an outmoded industrial age model. Therefore, from a teacher-centered perspective, what is of value is viewing schools and classrooms as workplaces. Classrooms are where laborers (students) are provided with standardized curricula and work hard to excel on objective assessments. Learning is viewed as the product of their efforts. Learning prepares them to enter the workforce.

Educators are evaluated based on their "laborers' time on task" and conformed work habits. Most importantly, they are held accountable for the results of their teaching (read as test scores). Schools are run like a business. The principal serves as the chief managerial officer who maintains a well-kept building and ensures "laborers" are always working. Thus, the teacher-centered story views schools as workplaces where managers (instructors) administer instructions to "laborers" to develop work habits and a strong work ethic to produce a product (knowledge).

TWENTY-FIRST-CENTURY CLASSROOM TEACHING PRACTICES: LEARNING AS PROCESS

Learner-Centered

Teachers perceive the need to:

- *view themselves as coaches, guides, or facilitators* who are coparticipants with their students in the learning process;
- monitor their amount of "talk" time so as *not to dominate classroom conversation and discussion*;
- *occasionally demonstrate* their curiosity, passion, and interest in students;
- *frequently display open-mindedness* and willingness to consider alternative perspectives;
- often take notice and *acknowledge* the thinking occurring in the classroom (e.g., Johnny is using mathematic reasoning to explain athe Pythagorean theorem);
- use *community-building language* (e.g., we, our);
- believe thinking *is* a "school as usual practice";
- ensure all students respect each other's thinking;
- challenge *ideas but not students*;
- make it easy for visitors to understand what the classroom educator cares about and values with respect to *learning*;
- show a genuine curiosity and interest in *learners' thinking*;
- listen in on groups and allow them to act *independently*;

- display and facilitate *thoughtful interactions, collaborations, and dialogue*;
- arrange classroom space to facilitate *thoughtful interactions*; and
- perceive schools and classrooms as *playscapes* within which learners develop and explore their mindscapes.

Teachers demonstrate the purpose of teaching by:

- conveying to students that the purpose of school is to *foster understanding*;
- demonstrating *thinking is central* to the lesson;
- providing sufficient time for learners to *process concepts*;
- focusing students' attention on essential ideas and *meaningful connections* of curriculum to world;
- providing opportunities for learners to use metacognitive thinking skills to plan, to monitor, as well as to *reflect on how their thinking has changed over time*;
- employing thinking routines effectively to deepen *students' understanding*;
- developing thinking routines that *further students' understanding* and as a venue for dialogue;
- utilizing a variety of teaching *deep processing thinking strategies* to aid students in organizing their thinking and deepening their understanding; and
- using qualitative and quantitative measures to gauge students' level of *understanding*.

Teachers encourage risk-taking by:

- *often taking learning risks* to demonstrate themselves as reflective learners;
- emphasizing that it's *good to take learning risks* even if you make mistakes;
- conveying to students that *mistakes are opportunities to learn*; and
- providing learners with *effort attributions* for success failure.

Teachers foster a meaningful approach to learning by:

- providing students with engaging personal growth opportunities to *develop competency in thinking skills and learning processes*;
- drawing upon effective routines and structures to help students organize their thinking using *higher-order thinking skills*;

- fostering competency in higher-order thinking skills of Bloom's taxonomy (e.g., understanding, analyzing, interpreting, creating, designing);
- demonstrating an authentic interest in and fostering students' *curiosity and thinking processes*;
- fostering the development of a *growth mindset*;
- making time for students' *questions and contributions*;
- *requiring students to model their thought processes* by providing evidence for their thinking;
- often using specific and targeted, *action-oriented feedback* that focuses on guiding future efforts and actions; and
- *typically demonstrating* their curiosity, passion, and interest in students.

Teachers create lessons that:

- provide their students with growth opportunities whereby they can direct their learning in becoming *teacher-independent learners*;
- provide learners with *rich thinking opportunities*;
- provide the time for students to *extend, elaborate, or develop ideas of others*;
- foster *learners' acquisition and mastery of cognitive and metacognitive learning skills*;
- foster *curiosity and collaboration*;
- provide students with opportunities to direct their own learning and *become independent learners*;
- provide group activities whereby students exchange ideas as they *work collaboratively* on assignments; and
- provide students with *open-ended learning assignments* with multiple outcomes.

Twenty-First-Century Educator Practices

In stark contrast, the student-centered twenty-first-century story views schools as places to develop, create, and innovate. The central values are *relationship and learning*, which will prepare them for a lifelong pursuit and love of learning. Toward this end, students engage in personal growth opportunities to develop competency in thinking skills and learning processes. These skills and processes promote the development of a growth mindset.

The major role of the principal is to serve as the school's educational leader. In this capacity, they champion their fellow educators in creating lessons that encourage meaningful approaches to learning and thinking. Educators view themselves as coaches, guides, or facilitators who are coparticipants with their students in the learning process. Classrooms are playscapes within which learners develop and explore their thought processes within mindscapes. Therefore, the new twenty-first-century learner-centered story is qualitatively distinct from the teacher-centered story.

SUMMARY

In the twentieth-century culture, economic progress and competition were valued in every aspect of society. In contrast, the emerging twenty-first-century paradigm is a quantum leap difference in what is valued. While economic progress is still a valued commodity, the twenty-first-century society has a vested interest in learning and personal growth. Individuals operating within this paradigm are motivated to learn for learning's sake alone. Learner-centered educators are highly process-oriented and regarded in their profession for their ability to envision and organize new and complex ideas from a variety of contexts (e.g., interdisciplinary). They are also visionary systems thinkers who can synthezie and integrate the ideas from multiple contexts to perceive innovative relationships. They value the diverse intelligences Howard Gardner has identified that are essential to flourish in the future. Thus, the shift in paradigm occurring at the opening of the twenty-first century involves a shift in values and thus has impacted all facets of our society. *The time has come to embrace the values and metaphors of the learner-centered Whole-Child story.*

Chapter Six

Toward a Constructivist Approach to Learning

The road to success is always under construction.—Anonymous

WHOLE-CHILD EDUCATION AND CONSTRUCTIVISM

The current framework is predicated on an outdated model for education. The school year is based on a now obsolete agrarian society's schedule for providing time to sow and reap agricultural harvests. The educational curricula are based on separate disciplines. The school day is divided up into forty-five- to sixty-minute time frames. The need to *conform* and the emphasis on teaching to "the test" are major roadblocks to fostering the imagination and innovation.

Robinson and Aronica (2015) eloquently related *creativity, innovation, and the imagination.*

> There are two other concepts to keep in mind: imagination and innovation. Imagination is the root of creativity. It is the ability to bring to mind things that aren't present to our senses. Creativity is putting your imagination to work. It is applied imagination. Innovation is putting new ideas into practice. (p. 118)

Therefore, what is needed now is to address students' individual learning needs rather than assuming they can all rise to the same level of expectations. This is particularly the case with respect to motivating students to learn in the first place. It is therefore essential that educators provide a safe and nonjudgmental classroom-learning environment. This is a classroom where teachers emphasize to their students that making mistakes is not a criticism of their lack of intelligence but an opportunity to learn. Being creative, innovative, and inventive should be our culture's measuring stick for being academically smart.

The school district's leadership has the responsibility to provide the educational vision and mission statements. This vision and mission provide a framework that specifies and addresses the needs of all students. However, the Whole-Child approach to teaching and learning requires classroom teachers to ultimately meet these needs.

This and the next three chapters will discuss the educator-based influences that affect the learning process. Moreover, they will discuss how and why these needs are best met by embracing a *constructivist* and *interdisciplinary approach* to teaching and learning. Nonetheless, occasionally there are times when employing an instructionist lesson is more appropriate. While this book advocates creating constructivist lessons, it should not be construed to entirely exclude instructionist ones. Therefore, deciding which type of lesson best fosters students' learning is up to the individual teacher.

Despite attempts to integrate Whole-Child educational practices, many educators typically adopt an *instructionist*, teacher-centered approach to learning. This approach views the teacher as an *instructor* who delivers a curriculum. Instructionist approaches provide students with only a superficial understanding (Brown et al., 2014). This approach only requires students to use low-order thinking skills (e.g., recalling, remembering, listing) (Chen & Yang, 2019). These thinking skills result in acquiring a shallow conceptual understanding. On the other hand, constructivist teachers require students to use higher-order thinking skills (e.g., elaborating, applying, modeling, etc.), which lead students to produce a deep conceptual understanding. Constructivist methodologies present the learner with opportunities to reconstruct and reorganize previously acquired knowledge in light of new experiences (Macy 1991).

The instructionist approach has dominated classroom teaching for many decades. It has led to the somewhat stereotyped perspective of teaching and classroom learning. This approach has been the target of educational reform efforts. The major difference between instructionist and constructivist approaches is that the former is concerned with *covering the curriculum* at the expense of fostering meaningful learning. The latter fosters the *development of a meaningful approach* to learning.

Sahlberg (2011) states that the globally distinguished Finnish education system doesn't emphasize "covering" the curriculum. Nonetheless, they continue to rank at the top of the Program for International Student Assessment (PISA) tests. Moreover, Sawyer (2019) states that not only do Finnish teachers cover less material, but they have fewer hours of instruction and homework.

Singapore, another high-ranking PISA educational system, focuses on fostering creativity. They replace the need to "cover" the curriculum with emphasizing core concepts, understanding, and criticial thinking (Singapore Ministry of Education, 2005, 2015). They also differ in the manner in which knowledge is acquired, stored, and retrieved, as well as in the types of skills required in performing these processes.

An instructionist perceives that the role of the learner and teacher is to acquire knowledge. A constructivist perceives the student and teacher as cocreators in the learning process. An instructionist educator perceives learners' knowledge issues as "pre-packaged" from their teaching. The constructivst educator perceives understanding to emerge from learners' active participation in the learning process. Therefore, constructivist educators provide learning experiences that promote opportunities for students to construct their own learning.

Mayer (1996) refers to educators as "guides" and learners as "sense makers." Gergen (1995) sees educators as coordinators, facilitators, resource advisors, tutors, or coaches. The constructivist approach requires that educators change their perspective of seeing their role as an authority figure.

Wagner (2012) states:

> Being the "sage on the stage" is problematic when you're trying to encourage intrinsic motivation and encourage students to have ownership of their learning. . . . It's hard to make the shift to being the "guide on the side," though. Giving up control is a huge issue for many teachers who are used to the old way. (pp. 162–163)

As discussed earlier, science education in the United States has recently unveiled its new and restructured K–12 standards in what is referred to as Next Generations Science Standards (NGSS). This new constructivist and process-based content standards frame what science students should learn and be able to do. Additionally, they foster science students to develop communication, collaboration, inquiry, problem solving, and learning skills. Central to the standards and subsequent curricular designs is *model-building*, which is a higher-order thinking process used by scientists.

Classroom implementation of the NGSS therefore requires constructivist practices described as:

1. making learning activities that include working on relevant problems,
2. creating lessons organized around "big ideas,"
3. seeking and valuing varied student perspectives,
4. creating learning events to engage all students, and
5. assessing student learning with respect to their "big picture" understanding in the context of reform teaching.

While these constructivist practices are central to the NGSS, they could be used in other disciplines as well.

GUIDED IMPROVISATION

Constructivist educators design lessons and activities that motivate and engage learners, as well as encourage them to take control of their learning. Sawyer (2019) maintains that one constructivist strategy—guided improvisation—bundles concepts into larger frameworks. These frameworks provide students with a deeper understanding than that gained from merely knowing the individual concepts. Therefore, constructivist strategies enable students to create a whole that is greater than the sum of its parts. Moreover, constructivist pedagogies foster creativity by encouraging learners to combine seemingly disparate concepts into a greater whole. Constructivist educators are also more likely to be able to integrate an interdisciplinary curriculum (Sawyer, 2019).

Sawyer (2019) describes guided improvisation as a learning strategy that expert educators use to foster learners' construction of creative knowledge. This strategy draws upon students' habits of mind to engage and guide learners in the construction of creative knowledge and a deep conceptual understanding. Sawyer cites habits of mind to include: *asking questions, being attentive in the problem space, being playful to try out new ideas, and taking time to experiment*. Hence, habits of mind typify constructivist thinking and problem solving.

As the editor of *The Cambridge Handbook of the Learning Sciences*, Sawyer attests to the fact that guided improvisation is an effective teaching strategy in teaching math and science. This teaching strategy is characterized by more open-ended lessons plans, since as experts, teachers can easily improvise as they flow through a lesson. Scaffolds to think and problem solve lie at the heart of constructivist strategies. Scaffolds are not arbitrary frameworks but rather well-thought-out guides to aid learners in solving a problem or developing deep conceptual understanding.

Thus, guided improvisation may be likened to how jazz musicians play off one another. While there is music to follow, jazz musicians do a lot of improvising by playing off the emergent riff of their fellow musicians. The same can be said for athletes playing a sport. While there are cleverly designed plays, implementation of them depends on several intangibles including how unpredictably the defense moves. Thus the ball carrier's actions are scaffolded by how his teammates react to the opponents.

Sawyer (2019) argues that using guided improvisation requires teachers to possess a deep conceptual understanding of their discipline. Moreover, since guided improvisation not only requires teachers to guide students but do so without a specific plan, constructivist teachers need to be creative. Toward this end, Sawyer offers seven habits of highly creative teachers. Creative teachers:

- allow students' actions to help guide the flow of the lesson,
- are willing to go off on tangents if it aids in the flow of the lesson,
- can work with cognitive dissonance to solve problems,
- are empathetic,
- integrate humor into their lessons,
- embrace reflective practice that enables them to review and adapt lessons, and
- view failures as learning opportunities.

SUMMARY

The Whole-Child framework offered here strives to contextualize learning by encouraging students to see and make connections, integrating learning in one area with that of another. Learning this way supports acquisition of higher reasoning skills, as well as critical and creative thinking abilities. From this new perspective, the learner is not perceived as someone disconnected from the learning environment. Rather, the learner is a participatory member of a *learning system* comprised of the teacher, students, and physical learning environment.

This learning system includes the *inter-objective* relationships between educator and district-based influences. However, and most importantly, are the *inter-subjective* exchanges that occur between learners and with their teachers (refer to figure 3.1).

Therefore, the Whole-Child educator challenges the traditional notion that classrooms need to operate according to the reason and logic of a rigid curriculum that predicts the learning outcome. Rather they recognize and promote learning by drawing from and building upon the insights of constructivist educators. Whole-Child educational processes foster the development of problem-solving abilities by raising students' awareness to other ways of thinking. Thus, fostering learning and thinking in the twenty-first-century classroom follows the Whole-Child education tradition in promoting constructivist strategies.

In essence, a constructivist approach to teaching and learning emphasizes the process of *creating* rather than merely *acquiring* knowledge. It also fosters the development of self-regulated learning behaviors that encourage students to take a more meaningful approach to learning. Studies measuring the efficacy of constructivist versus instructionist approaches to teaching and learning have concluded that the former are much more effective in fostering achievement (Adak, 2017).

Moreover, constructivist practices promote knowledge retention (Narli, 2011) and transfer (Resnick, 1989) to other situations. A meaningful approach to teaching promotes understanding. Moreover, a deeper and more integrated web of conceptual relationships characterizes this understanding. Instructionist, or rote learning, approaches typically employ only surface learning strategies. In contrast, a meaningful approach to learning draws upon deeper learning strategies like elaboration, critical thinking, and self-regulation.

Constructivist educators, in direct contrast to instructionist educators, routinely utilize thinking routines to help their students organize their thinking and deepen their level of understanding. Thus conceptual understanding is more likely to develop in a constructivist setting where students use learning strategies to learn and solve problems.

Chapter Seven

What Thinking Skills Foster Meaningful Learning

I never teach my pupils; I only attempt to provide the conditions in which they can learn.—Albert Einstein

TEACHER-CENTERED VERSUS WHOLE-CHILD LEARNING

In chapter 4, we discussed the major differences between the metaphors of the twentieth-century or teacher-centered and the twenty-first-century and the learner-centered Whole-Child story. The former values, perceives, and declares *learning as a product* assessed by the extent to which knowledge is acquired by students. The latter values and fosters *learning as a process* whereby learners are encouraged to take a meaningful approach to their studies.

It is interesting to note that "product" is a noun while "to process" is a verb. Therefore, the teacher-centered perspective is static and passive while the Whole-Child perspective is dynamic and active. Thus, project/problem-based learning fosters an active and engaging approach to learning and thinking and, as such, is a constructivst and more meaningful way to learn and think.

Unfortunately teacher-centered educators employ instructionist-teaching strategies that encourage rote approaches to learning. In fairness to this approach, they feel pressured to prepare students for national or state-mandated standardized tests. Nonetheless, this occurs despite all the research concluding enhanced achievement and test performance for students who develop meaningful approaches to learning (Novak, 1998).

It is problematic for educators to adopt meaningful approaches when the "educational system" has indoctrinated students to use rote approaches. This was well pointed out by Kinchin (2001): "A curriculum that is designed to be learnt by rote . . . provides little incentive for educators to encourage their students to engage in more meaningful learning" (p. 1265).

ENCOURAGING MEANINGFUL LEARNING AND THINKING

Meaningful learning consists of applying learning strategies to "hands-on" and "minds-on" experiences that challenge preconceived assumptions and understanding. These learning experiences create a disparity between what learners observe and their present level of understanding. It is here that the *Whole-Child constructivist educator* can make a real difference in motivating learners to reconstruct their level of understanding.

The Whole-Child educator embraces the notion that any individual can learn a given subject if provided with scaffolded learning experiences and a conducive (read as caring and compassionate) environment. Meaningful learning and thinking processes encourage learners to actively participate in their own learning. Learning, and therefore meaning, is constructed from learners' own efforts. Additionally, holistic and integrated approaches to learning and thinking are essential to the building of higher-order thinking and habits of mind.

Moreover, the possibility exists that learning within interdisciplinary frameworks not only fosters *creativity* but *attentiveness*. The notion offered here is that *individuals provided with learning opportunities in an interactive, integrated, and interdisciplinary environment will become more effective and successful problem solvers, thinkers, and learners.*

In their book *A New Culture of Learning*, Douglas Thomas and John Seely Brown (2011) define what they refer to as *arc-of-life learning*. This defines learning as that which continues throughout our lives. Thomas and Seely Brown make a strong case for capitalizing on digital technologies in ushering in a new culture of learning. This culture enhances learning processes through online resources to play, question, and imagine new ideas.

Their new culture of learning is based on three principles:

1. Develop teaching and learning approaches to thrive in a rapidly changing world.
2. Develop and integrate digital technologies that foster user-friendly peer-to-peer learning.
3. Capitalize on peer-to-peer digital learning to shape the collective learning process between several collaborating learners.

Thomas and Seely Brown further contend that knowledge developed in the twentieth-century classroom was *explicit* and therefore easily evaluated with objective assessments. However, in the twenty-first century, knowledge is becoming *tacit* (e.g., doing, observing, and experiencing) and not amenable to objective assessments. Rather digital portfolios and project presentations are more apt in capturing the essence of students' work. In the twenty-first-century classroom, textbooks are no longer stable resources due to the fact that knowledge is rapidly changing.

Digital technologies are making it easier to develop and transmit new knowledge acquired by a growing number of online users. It is quite possible that learners, in the not so distant future, will exclusively use computers, rather than textbooks, to gather and exchange information. If educators truly value meaningful learning, they will offer learning opportunities that provide students with open-ended learning experiences.

Students will more fully engage in projects where they can explore topics they are passionate about. As discussed in chapter 2, currently many educators are using PBL to foster critical thinking and problem-solving abilities. PBL provides learners with open-ended, real-world problems and opportunities to pose potential solutions to those problems. Furthermore, it fosters collaboration, research, critical thinking, problem solving, and metacognition thinking skills.

PBL also provides learners with opportunities to learn how to overcome challenging obstacles. The project's proposed question drives students to make their own decisions, research, and review their process. Darling-Hammond et al. (2008) concluded that "when students engage in PBL, their motivation is higher than in an instructionist classroom" (p. 42).

Michael Polyani (as discussed in Brownhill, 1981) coined the term "indwelling" to refer to becoming familiar with inquiry processes to the extent that they become second nature. Indwelling makes the tacit dimensions of knowledge (e.g., discovering, exploring) more accessible. In so doing, it enables the learner to discover relationships between various knowledge sources. Hence, learners collaborating on PBL projects promote a collective indwelling of learning and thinking skills. Nonetheless, since learners typically have their own idiosyncratic ways of learning, assessing learning can be a challenge for the twenty-first-century educator. Therefore, creating qualitative rubrics would provide a more effective and valid means to assess projects.

WHAT ARE THE LEARNING AND THINKING SKILLS NEEDED TO THRIVE IN THE TWENTY-FIRST CENTURY?

Recent findings from research studies conducted by neuroscientists, developmental psychologists, and educational motivational theorists support strategies that foster the development of the *whole child*. Reason together with emotion has provided today's educator with a totally new perspective of how we think and learn. *Redesigning the curriculum* around *project-based learning* would go a long way toward fostering several of the skills cited as essential for success in the twenty-first century.

Wagner (2012) emphasizes that educators need to take a fresh perspective on how they perceive knowledge and its usage:

> Increasingly in the twenty-first century, what you know is far less important than what you can do with what you know. The interest in and ability to create new knowledge to solve new problems is the single most important skill that all students must master today. (p. 142)

Similarly, in his book *A Whole New Mind* (2005), best-selling author Daniel Pink argues that affluence, technology, and globalization have transformed our culture. This transformation has resulted in a shift from left-brain (i.e., L-Directed) thinking to thinking including right-brain (i.e., R-Directed) processes. Rather than diminishing the importance of L-Directed thought processes, Pink argues for augmenting those by including R-Directed processes.

Pink refers to right-brain skills as "high concept" or "high touch." High concept refers to the ability to use one's aesthetic sensibility to make insightful discoveries and use them in creating and innovating. High touch abilities provide a capacity to empathize with others and find personal meaning and purpose in one's work.

In their book, *That Used to Be Us: How America Fell Behind in the World It Invented and How We Can Come Back,* Thomas Friedman and Michael Mandelbaum (2011) implore today's educators to take up the gauntlet for educating today's youth:

> The world increasingly will be divided between high imagination-enabling countries, which encourage and enable the imagination and extras of the people, and low imagination-enabling countries, which suppress or simply fail to develop their people's creative capacities and abilities to spark new ideas, start up new industries and nurture their own "extra." (p. 138)

Thus, as Pink (2005) asserts, there are twenty-first-century forces—*abundance, automation, and outsourcing routine white-collar jobs to Asia*—that have tipped the scales in favor of developing R-Directed thinking attributes. L-Directed thinking occupations like engineering and manufacturing are diminishing while R-Directed thinking occupations like entrepreneurs and innovators are growing. The conceptual age is changing which skills and knowledge schools need to be fostering in order for graduates to find success in the twenty-first-century marketplace. Pink (2005) offers six "senses" required to thrive in the conceptual age: design, story, symphony, empathy, play, and meaning.

Design

Apple is an ideal company to exemplify the importance of design. Apple's products, from their iPods, iPads, and desk and laptop computers to their watches and packaging, are sleek, eye-catching, elegant, innovative, creative, and technologically cutting-edge, as well as functional.

Story

Surviving in the advertising world requires companies to develop a brand-driven story to market their products. Today's consumers of big-tag items like automobiles want a story that provides a meaningful understanding of a company's values. Ultimately, a company's story may very well result in the purchase of one company's product over another. Such is the case for Ford Motor Company (Butkevicius, 2019): "A good story makes you feel something and is universal. They want to grasp your values and your commitment to excellence; be inspired and intrigued. Storytelling is the most powerful way to convey these ideas" (Mark Truby, vice president of the Ford Motor Company).

A growing number of companies have developed a story to market their wares:

- The global online rental property Airbnb asks patrons to post their own stories to market their residences.
- Goodlife Fitness has replaced its high-pressure sales tactics of the past and visuals of impossibly trim and toned bodies with a story that appeals to the regular person seeking better physical and mental health.
- Burt's Bees' story explains that the husband and wife founders met each other on a hiking expedition and decided to make wax candles together.
- Nike started its branding story using super athlete Michael Jordan as the focus of a Nike commercial. Who wouldn't want to buy something that Jordan touts? Since then nearly everything Nike does or makes is accompanied by a story.

Symphony

Many white-collar analytical professions are now outsourced to Asia. Therefore, professions that require synthesizing are growing in demand. While analyzing is a L-Directed thinking skill, synthesizing is a R-Directed thinking skill. Music composers, entrepreneurs, graphic artists, and inventors draw upon the ability to synthesize. Advertising requires "high touch" synthesizers who can create an eye-catching phrase, logo, or metaphor to represent a product. The astute observer of the FedEx logo can see in the white space between the "E" and "x" a white arrow.

Thriving in the conceptual age requires being able to make connections between disciplines—thinking across disciplines (interdisciplinary). Holistic healers (e.g., naturopaths, chiropractors, acupuncturists, osteopaths), unlike traditional allopathic practitioners, make diagnoses and treat patients from a holistic mind/body perspective. Therefore, they need to be great synthesizers who rely more on understanding the big (holistic) picture to treat their patients. Professions in the twenty-first century, especially those that demand creativity, are requiring crossing boundaries between disciplines. Hence the days of teaching students from separate disciplines no longer will work in the conceptual age. Sawyer (2019) asserts his term "creative knowledge" is similar in meaning to other terms used by Darling-Hammond et al. (2008) and three-dimensional learning (NGSS, 2014).

Empathy

Empathy is an R-Directed thinking capability to understand how another person feels. Empathy is critical in forming lasting and meaningful relationships (e.g., mother-child; husband-wife): "What will distinguish those who thrive will be their ability to understand what makes their fellow man or woman tick, to forge relationships, and to care for others" (Pink, 2005, p. 66).

As will be discussed in a subsequent chapter, emotional intelligence, as defined by Daniel Goleman in his best-selling book *Emotional Intelligence* (1995), is an aptitude for feeling empathy. Children on the autism spectrum tend to be socially compromised because they can have difficulty with empathy. Interestingly, all mammals possess a unique set of "mirror" neurons in a facial recognition area of their frontal lobe that enable them to literally mimic what another individual is feeling (Pink, 2005).

Play

Play is a universal, cross-cultural, and necessary attribute of people of all ages. All mammals have an innate tendency to play as youthful beings. Play is a developmental process whereby relationships develop along with neural pathways that the organisms will draw upon later in life. Play is essential for learning. Almost all the learning that goes on in the first years of life is in the context of exploration of the environment. Thomas and Seely Brown (2011) suggest that play provides learners with the opportunity to explore new ideas and ways of doing without a concern for failing. One of their most profound statements regarding integrating play into adulthood (and not only childhood) is: "Play, questioning, and—perhaps most important—imagination lie at the very heart of arc-of-life learning" (p. 2). Hence they believe that play is critical for transitioning to an educational approach that best prepares students for life and success in the twenty-first century.

Furthermore, Siyahhan and Gee (2018) emphasize the importance of play in development and the learning process:

> Children use play and imagination as the primary mechanisms for making sense of their new, rapidly evolving world. In other words, as children encounter new places, people, things, and ideas, they use play and imagination to cope with the massive influx of information they receive. (p. 19)

The importance of play is not a new idea. In his classic text *Mind in Society*, social constructivist Lev Vygotsky (1978) stated, "A child's greatest achievements are possible in play, achievements that tomorrow will become her basic level of real action and morality" (p. 102). Therefore, these investigators are asking educators to reconsider integrating play into classroom learning to foster creativity and innovative thinking. This is especially true for the cognitive, emotional, and social development of children (Ginsburg, 2007).

It is through play that children come to explore their world, negotiate, and resolve conflicts (Erickson, 1985). Play is also a means for stimulating creativity and innovation and viewing problems from different perspectives, which is critical for any creative field of endeavor. While play is certainly essential for children, it actually is important throughout one's adult life (Robinson et al., 2019). Play:

- relieves stress,
- improves brain function,
- refreshes your mind and body,
- encourages teamwork,
- triggers creativity and innovation,
- enables you to view problems differently,
- stimulates the mind and boosts creativity,
- improves relationships and your connection to others, and
- keeps you feeling young and energetic.

Meaning

Ronald Ingelhart (1997, as cited in Pink, 2005) provides insight into the importance of meaning in the conceptual age: "a gradual shift from Materialist values (emphasizing economic and physical security above all) toward Post-materialist priorities (emphasizing self-expression and the quality of life)" (p. 219).

Meaning has become central to our lives. Therefore, it behooves the Whole-Child educator to create lessons that provide students with opportunities to create an understanding of themselves. As will be discussed in a subsequent chapter, research emerging from Positive Psychology suggests *meaning* is critical for individuals to experience happiness. Moreover, an abundance of research studies substantiate the claim that those who lack meaning and purpose in their lives are more prone to psychopathological illness like depression (Steger, 2012).

Meaning is central to developing a sense of purpose in our lives. Meaning emerges *"from the web of connections, interpretations, aspirations*, and evaluations that (1) make our experiences comprehensible, (2) direct our efforts toward desired futures, and (3) provide a sense that our lives matter and are worthwhile" (italics added, Martela & Steger, 2016, p. 538). Therefore Pink's six "senses" are deemed essential to thrive in the twenty-first century and, as such, need to be integrated into school curricula fostering a more meaningful approach to learning.

In *Five Minds for the Future*, educational guru Howard Gardner (2006) offers a different perspective regarding the thinking skills of today's learners. Gardner states that educators need to consider these skills to ensure today's youth are able to thrive and flourish in the twenty-first century. Gardner conceives of five different kinds of minds: disciplined, synthesizing, creating, respectful, and ethical.

The Disciplined Mind

Learners with a disciplined mind persistently strive to develop competence in, and understanding of, the skills and content of a particular subject discipline. Therefore, as the name implies, the disciplined student has a strong work ethic and adopts a growth mindset. Gardner asserts that one of the major concerns with students taught from instructionist approaches is that they merely *acquire* numerous facts and concepts. The critique from cognitive researchers is that learning this way doesn't produce a coherent and deep understanding of a subject.

The Synthesizing Mind

Conversely, the ability to learn in a disciplined manner provides the learner with a deeper understanding. This is particularly the case if they utilize the synthesizing mind to make new connections. Therefore, *it is plausible to suggest that constructivist strategies should foster development of a disciplined mind.* The disciplined mind is especially important for the future because solving interdisciplinary problems is becoming essential in understanding how complex systems work.

With a deep understanding of several disciplines, the disciplined mind can analyze problems that arise and effectively address and resolve them. Similarly to Pink's symphony, Gardner's synthesizing mind enables the learner to perceive meaningful relationships between seemingly unrelated concepts.

The Creative Mind

The creating mind, like the synthesizing mind, is able to provide learners with a unique and novel perspective that provides them with a broader understanding. Like the disciplined mind, thinking synthetically will be essential in order to solve problems in an interdisciplinary context. Today experts from a variety of disciplines work together to create new designs and solve complex problems.

For instance, humankind is now facing a global warming crisis that can only be resolved from an interdisciplinary approach. Climatologists can explain how increasing burning of fossil fuels creates a rise in mean global temperature and melting of the ice caps. Water and atmospheric scientists weigh in on how global temperature is controlled by the amount of carbon dioxide taken up by the oceans, as well as land and aquatic plants.

Ecologists can discuss how pollution affects land and aquatic ecosystems that, in turn, affect the amount of carbon dioxide in the atmosphere. Politicians need to be able to comprehend the advice from all these scientific experts in order to make legislative changes. Civil engineers discuss how to contend with a rising sea level. Economists analyze the effects to the nation's economy if legislative bills mandate changes in fossil fuel usage.

In summary, we now live in a global society and therefore problems have become worldwide in nature. Thus the synthesizing and disciplined minds are critically needed to creatively problem solve issues on a global scale. It is from this interdisciplinary approach that a new solution can emerge that has a wider breadth of explanatory power to understand the myriad factors impacting the behavior of complex systems.

The Respectful Mind

The respectful mind is critical for being able to tolerate and accept, if not celebrate, cultural differences in order to live and work in a global society. America is the cultural "melting pot" of the world. Therefore, Americans have been challenged with respecting differences in social mores, cultural practices, and religious affiliations, to name but a few. Politics and economics are no longer locally focused. Rather legislative decisions are made in a context of different nationalities, faiths, and political regimes. This requires policy makers to respect others and make ethical decisions to do what is in the best interests for the majority of people.

The Ethical Mind

The ethical mind situates behaviors and ambitions in the context of unselfishly enhancing the needs, aspirations, and benefit of society. One case in point was the air pollution crisis in Sweden. Sweden is not an industrial giant that creates air pollution. Swedish scientists determined that their air pollution originated in industrial England and was subsequently being carried easterly to Sweden. Consequently, Sweden sued Britain and mandated they reduce their air pollution. This required the creation of a new type of legal set of rights—international law.

Behaving in an ethical manner lies at the heart of the legal, medical, political, and educational professions. An individual can actually lose their license and be fired for acting in an unethical manner. However, ethical behavior is expected in all professions. You implicitly expect a plumber, electrician, carpenter, or mason to provide the service you hired them to perform. If they don't, you can report them to their union. This also holds true for businesses. If they commit fraud or endanger the public, they become subject to lawsuits. Therefore, the ethical mind is one that all citizens need to develop.

In *The Global Achievement Gap*, Tony Wagner (2008) states U.S. high schools graduate a lower percentage of students relative to other developed nations. Moreover, many graduates are ill-prepared for success in postsecondary institutions. Wagner makes a strong argument for transcending the old three Rs of the past and integrating other thinking skills into the system that promote success in the twenty-first century.

In *Most Likely to Succeed* (2015), Wagner and Dintersmith cite the following essential skills to flourish in the twenty-first century:

- critical thinking,
- problem solving,
- collaboration,
- agility and adaptability,

- initiative and entrepreneurialism,
- communication skills,
- the ability to analyze information, and
- curiosity and imagination.

Of highest priority is teaching learners how to think. Thus, strategies that foster *problem-solving*, *critical thinking*, and *higher-order thinking* skills need to become the new norm in American classrooms. Companies and firms are challenging their employees to *collaborate* on projects due to the fact that designing, synthesizing, and creating new products require teams of people. Effectively *communicating*, both orally and in written form, is a skill for which competence needs to be developed by *all* students. In the past, high school or college graduates typically prepared for a specific career path or undertook a liberal arts education. Most worked in a specific occupation for most of their lives. However, today, as a result of technological advances, careers are emerging more rapidly than schools can prepare their students to enter.

Heather Long (2016) refers to the "new normal" for today's millennial generation as one where they can expect to change careers four times before they reach the age of thirty-two. Therefore, today's youth will need to develop *agility* and *adaptability* to quickly change careers or take on completely new roles in a career in a fast-paced and changing future. The shift from the nineteenth century to the twenty-first century was a change from an industrial age to the digital age. Twentieth-century schools maintained the values and structure of the nineteenth century. However, the world has changed, and education needs to change with it. *Initiative* and *entrepreneurship* are two qualities requisite for thriving in the rapidly changing world of the digital age.

Few and far between are the erstwhile "Mom and Pop" shops that were passed down to children. Today new businesses crop up all the time while those of the past disappear. Therefore, individuals who want to thrive in the Whole-Child era need to be *curious* and *imaginative* to create and fill new business niches that will grow and prosper. Moreover, to be *entrepreneurial* and take *initiative*, in many cases, requires having to learn a new skill set. Needless to say, careers in the digital age require employees to be able to *analyze*, *interpret*, and *communicate* enormous amounts of information.

A case in point is in understanding how the typical middle or high school student sets out to write a research paper. Most, if not all, immediately go to the Internet. Fact finding on the Internet is a dubious pursuit. With the exception of refereed journal articles, there isn't a panel of experts who judges the merit and authenticity of what one finds on the Internet. Therefore, instructing students to use primary and authentic sources is essential.

In their comprehensive work *Learning and Leading With Habits of Mind: 16 Essential Characteristics for Success*, Arthur Costa and Bena Kallick (2008, p. xx–xxi) posited sixteen habits of learning. These habits of mind aid students in successfully approaching and solving problems they may encounter in their classroom assignments and everyday life. Therefore, these can and need to be integrated into the curriculum. The sixteen habits of mind include:

- managing impulsivity;
- persisting;
- listening to others with understanding and empathy;
- thinking flexibly;
- thinking about thinking (metacognition);
- striving for accuracy and precision;
- thinking and communicating with clarity and precision;
- questioning and posing problems;
- applying past knowledge to new situations;
- gathering data through all the senses;
- taking responsible risks;
- creating, imagining, and innovating;
- thinking interdependently;
- finding humor;
- responding with wonderment and awe; and
- learning continuously.

Similarly, Education Reimagined (2015) asserts that for today's youth to thrive in the twenty-first century, learning dispositions need to be reconsidered (p. 6). Learning dispositions foster engaging in challenging learning tasks. Additionally, these traits predispose individuals to engage and actively participate in ethical and socially relevant issues. These learning dispositions include:

- agency (self-efficacy),
- curiosity,
- initiative,
- resilience,
- adaptability,
- persistence,
- leadership,
- ethical behavior,
- self-control, and
- civic responsibility.

This raises the question: *where and how are these twenty-first-century skills and meaningful learning processes being taught?* The section that follows features two exemplary schools, each of whom are at the cutting edge of educating students for success in the twenty-first century.

TWENTY-FIRST-CENTURY EXEMPLAR SCHOOLS

New Technology High School, Napa, California

In his article on New Technology High School, Bob Pearlman (2006) asks the question: "How do they learn it? How do students know they know it? And what do schools look like where 21st century learning takes place?" (p. 102). In short, Pearlman's answer to these questions is New Technology High School (NTHS) in Napa, California. A cadre of business leaders, educators, and civic leaders who sought to use America's educational best practices to create a new school that incorporated them founded NTHS. The school has eight learning outcomes that are assessed by students creating a digital portfolio: content standards, collaboration, critical thinking, oral communications, written communication, career preparation, citizenship and ethics, and technology literacy (Pearlman, 2006).

NTHS bases its instruction around project- and problem-based learning. Projects are designed to address real-world complex issues that require deep processing, rigor, and use of higher-order thinking skills to complete. Each project is framed by eight learning outcomes:

1. to learn *collaboration*, work in teams;
2. to learn *critical thinking*, take on complex problems;
3. to learn *oral communication*, present;
4. to learn *written communication*, write;
5. to learn *technology*, use technology;
6. to develop *citizenship*, take on civic and global issues;
7. to learn about *careers*, do internships; and
8. to learn *content*, research and do all of the above. (italics mine, Pearlman, 2006, pp. 104–105)

What NTHS staff do that is critical for effective project designs and completion is providing ongoing *constructive feedback* on students' progress. The project/problem-based learning is primarily the responsibility of the student. Nonetheless, any project requires some guidance along the path from inception to completion. The teacher provides constructive feedback that motivates students and helps them move forward to the next stage in the process. In this regard, teachers are *guides or mentors* for students rather than assuming the traditional role as *instructor*.

In contrast to traditional programs, NTHS doesn't grade students with a single letter grade. Rather they assess students on the basis of the learning outcomes of their project, which is more authentic and meaningful. What follows is Pearlman's (2006) advice to educators:

> Countries need to upgrade their educational standards to world-class standards; moving curriculum to 100 percent in-depth project- and problem-based learning that involves teamwork, critical thinking, and communication skills; authentically assessing for learning all these skills for immediate and active feedback to students. (p. 111)

Francis W. Parker School, Chicago, Illinois

The Francis W. Parker School in Chicago, Illinois, bases its raison d'être on John Dewey's principles of Whole-Child education summarized with his aphorism: "Education does not prepare one for life. Education is life." Parker's five core goals are represented by the anagram TIDES wherein T is technology, I is innovation, D is design, E is entrepreneurship, and S is society (Moran, 2006). Students' work is framed by this five-letter anagram with the explicit goal to develop interdisciplinary learning experiences that prepare each student to thrive in the twenty-first century.

Francis W. Parker's TIDES re-envisions education in the context of the twenty-first-century digital age. Each day students and staff alike consider what they can do to motivate themselves to make an impact on the world. Design is not only central to Parker's students' projects but issues from empathy:

> Design thinking is a way to use empathy to understand and analyze a variety of solutions to solve both big and small problems. . . . Design thinking offers a way—through the iterative process—to use that empathy to create something new and unique for others. (Moran 2006, p. 84)

Parker's students are instructed in the art of entrepreneurship by pursuing growth opportunities. For some these include developing a business plan and presenting their idea to potential investors—reminiscent of an episode on TV's *Shark Tank*. Similar to NTHS's main outcome goal, the entrepreneurial aspect of the Parker program fosters students with the knowledge, skills, and dispositions to directly impact the world.

SUMMARY

This chapter began with an indictment of the current American educational ethos, despite piecemeal reforms that have left nothing new in their wake. The thrust of this chapter was to make a strong case to transform rather than merely reform education by envisioning a new educational framework with its focus on a learner-centered approach to teaching. It is easy to appreciate why Education Reimagined's learning dispositions, Costa and Kallick's habits of mind, Pink's "senses," Gardner's "minds," and Wagner's skills need to be integrated into school curricula to prepare today's youth for today's digital age.

It befits any educator to find ways to impress upon students the value of embracing them. If educators want their students to develop a deep understanding of subject matter, they need to foster a more meaningful approach to learning at as early an age as possible. Adopting a more constructivist approach to classroom teaching can facilitate this. Constructive approaches to learning place the responsibility of meaning making in the minds of the students rather than in the "chalk-talk" of educators' lecture presentations. It also means assessing students on the basis of their depth of understanding rather than on rote memorization of facts.

In a six-year longitudinal study, Marcon (2002) concluded that students whose preschool experience was based on constructivist methods demonstrated significantly higher grades in later elementary years than those who experienced instructionist methods. Furthermore, she suggested that the difference was most likely due to the former promoting higher motivation, independence, and self-initiated learning. Collectively these led to a higher use of critical thinking and comprehension skills in later years.

The Whole-Child educator has a vested interest in preparing students for life in the twenty-first century. Therefore, it is vital that they integrate skills, learning dispositions and habits of mind, and practices into their classroom teaching. The outcome of these changes provides teachers with a renewed vision of their mission to foster the growth and development of *authentic learners*. In conclusion, *Whole-Child educators adopt constructivist practices that foster the use and development of higher-order learning and metacognitive thinking skills. Consequently, their efforts support students in adopting a more meaningful approach to learning and thinking.* A twenty-first-century learner-centered approach also integrates an interdisciplinary curriculum. This is the subject of the following chapter.

Chapter Eight

The Interdisciplinary Curriculum

> *To develop a complete mind: study the science of art; study the art of science. Learn how to see. Realize that everything connects to everything else.*
> —Leonardo da Vinci

TRUTH, BEAUTY, AND GOODNESS

Every culture has constructed their societies on the pillars of the Platonic triad of what is true, what is beautiful, and what is good. In *Truth, Beauty and Goodness Reframed: Educating for the Virtues in the Twenty-First Century*, Howard Gardner (2011) asks, "Why should we care about the true, the beautiful and the good?" (p. 4). The sciences have provided what is true; the arts and humanities have defined what is beautiful; and the government and legal bodies have determined what is good.

Science and mathematics have provided us with a high quality of life due to innovative developments in medicine, transportation, and communication. The arts and humanities have provided us with the means to explore and develop our aesthetic sense whereby we can creatively express ourselves. And the social sciences have provided humankind with a sense of what is moral and ethical in relating to others.

Thus, individuals have three different realms—or what are referred to as disciplines—that impact their learning. A well-rounded liberal arts education consists of courses in science, math, the arts, humanities, and social sciences. However, these realms are artificial and therefore are not independent disciplines. Therefore, what is suggested here is that today's educational curriculum needs to provide learners with an interdisciplinary combination of all of five disciplines.

THE ARTS: A BRIDGE TO INTERDISCIPLINARY LEARNING

The "arts" are defined and created by a culture's sense of the aesthetic. It is in this sense that Whole-Child educators are practitioners of the *art of teaching* and abide by the following:

- Learning occurs in integrated and interdisciplinary contexts.
- Teachers use constructivist pedagogies.
- Teaching is an "art."
- Teachers are the "guide on the side."
- Teachers foster students taking a meaningful approach to learning.
- Learning takes place using online resources to augment teachers' multimedia presentations.
- Assignments are project-based over extended periods of time.
- E-books serve as course resources.
- Learning is "active" and typically conducted in collaborative groups using advances in technology.
- Teaching is learning-focused.
- Teachers are facilitators.
- Teachers implement an integrated curriculum.
- Teachers evaluate with self-assessments and formative assessments.
- Teachers hold high expectations.

Arts educators have laid claim to the notion that the arts are essential to not only a child's academic and social education but also their skills transfer to other disciplines:

> A growing body of studies, including those in the research compendium *Critical Evidence* [*How the Arts Benefit Student Achievement*] presents compelling evidence . . . [that] document the habits of mind, social competencies and personal dispositions inherent to arts learning. Additionally, research has shown that what students learn in the arts may help them to master other subjects, such as reading, math or social studies. (Ruppert, 2006 p. 8)

Elliott Eisner (2002), one of the most passionate advocates of the arts in education, believes that the serious study and practice of an artistic discipline is the most effective way for children to learn the following:

1. Making judgments entails more than drawing upon rational thought and logic. Rather "rightness of fit," which depends on our sensibility or feeling, also needs to be considered.
2. The arts teach children that there can be more than one answer to a question.

3. The arts offer opportunities for each student to express their unique perspective.
4. The arts teach children that complex problems typically have solutions that are not easily recognized. Therefore, problem solving requires persistence, remaining open-minded, and being willing to concede initial explanations and vigilantly look for alternative answers as they immerse themselves in the problem space.
5. The arts teach us that literal language and quantification do not exclusively limit the depth of understanding. Rather representing or expressing one's feelings is just as valid.
6. The arts teach students that no matter how insignificant their contribution may seem, it might have a ripple effect and notably affect others to produce a significant effect.
7. The arts teach students the importance of the imagination in thinking through a situation or problem. New ideas emerge as "images," which then may foster different and more productive ways of thinking.
8. The arts help children learn to express how something makes them feel. In so doing, they learn to discover words to express their feelings and aesthetic impressions.
9. The arts teach that relationships between the "parts" enable us to understand the "whole." This is true whether it is a poem, artwork, mathematical theorem, political policy, or scientific principle.
10. The arts teach us there are three reasons to undertake something: the quality, the value, and/or the rewards it affords us.

This is exactly why Eisner has endeared himself to educators far and wide, especially those outside the arts. It is for this reason that the arts used to have a more dominant role and should again play a central role in early childhood education. Pink and Gardner would concur with this recommendation. Unfortunately, the arts have been swept under the rug because they are not recognized as "academic" disciplines.

Nonetheless, many believe the arts are *more* important than the so-called academic subjects to success as adults. Moreover, as a direct consequence of Eisner's influence, many believe the arts should *also* be considered "core" subjects. In fact, some would go so far as to say that the arts are actually fundamental to all other disciplines.

Fortunately, some schools have incorporated the arts into their science, technology, engineering, and math (STEM) interdisciplinary approach. Thus, the arts were adding to STEM by changing the acronym to STEAM (adding A for arts to the acronym). STEAM was developed to provide science students with the skills, creativity, aesthetic sensibility, as well as knowledge critical to flourish in tomorrow's marketplace.

Educators across the world have argued for creating a more balanced interdisciplinary approach to teaching that includes the humanities. Toward this end, they suggest adding an H to the STEAM acronym (SHTEAM) (Connor et al., 2015). The thrust of their rationale is to provide students with a much wider scope of skill sets to promote an enhanced ability to problem-solve (Winterman and Malacinski, 2015). Quigley and Herro (2016) state: "The goal of this approach is to prepare students to solve the world's pressing issues through innovation, creativity, critical thinking, effective communication, collaboration, and ultimately new knowledge" (p. 1).

STEAM is designed to present students with multiple ways to problem-solve in an interdisciplinary context. Moreover, some more philosophically inclined educators (Watson and Watson, 2013) have argued that the rift between science and the humanities failed to consider the merit of "art and imagination." Other Whole-Child educators have advocated for STEAM from the perspective that doing so increases learner motivation, engagement, and more effective discipline learning of STEM courses (Henrkisen et al., 2015). STEAM curricula enable students to make connections between different disciplines (Connor, Karmokar, and Whittington, 2015).

In addition to mastering the skills of the core disciplines the Partnership for 21st Century Learning (2011) maintains that schools must integrate twenty-first-century interdisciplinary themes into core subjects.

Twenty-first-century themes include:

- global awareness;
- financial, economic, business, and entrepreneurial literacy;
- civic literacy;
- health literacy; and
- environmental literacy.

The Partnership for 21st Century Learning (2011) document acknowledges the research that problem solving has a social dimension that offers enriching learning opportunities. The International Society for Technology in Education (ISTE) recommends the following during K–12 education (2015):

- creating, achieving, and demonstrating personal learning goals;
- providing students with opportunities to become digitally literate;
- fostering students in drawing from a variety of digital resources to construct knowledge and take a meaningful approach to learning;
- using a variety of digital tools and resources to become innovative designers in the digital landscape;
- utilizing a variety of strategies to solve problems and demonstrate the power of technology to test solutions;
- demonstrating competency in effectively communicating; and

- collaborating with others in local and global contexts.

The arts and humanities add what Pink (2005) refers to as "high-concept" R-Directed thinking (e.g., design, story, and symphony) that augments the learning process. According to Maeda (2013), "Design creates the innovative products and solutions that will propel our economy forward, and artists ask the deep questions about humanity that reveal which way forward actually is" (p. 34). Thus, STEAM and SHTEAM frameworks answer Wagner's (2012), Pink's (2005), and Gardner's (2006) claims to the types of skills requisite to flourish in the twenty-first century. A Whole-Child, interdisciplinary, and constructivist approach together with the twenty-first-century skill set will better prepare learners to thrive in the future. Therefore, teacher preparation courses and professional development for veteran educators need to evolve. Today's educators need to understand how to integrate more right-brain strengths and experiential approaches to thinking into classroom teaching.

SUMMARY

The curricular framework structured around an interdisciplinary learning style is considerably different from traditional ones. Traditionally, educational goals speak to educating the whole person but seldom do so. Delivering learning in discipline-based courses results in students perceiving knowledge as divided up into separate classifications. As a result, students come to believe they can only understand the world by studying independent discipline-based courses. However, nothing could be further from the truth. Dividing up knowledge into separate disciplines is a consequence of the reductionist thinking harking back to the mid- to late nineteenth century.

All knowledge realms are interrelated. Therefore, discipline-based thinking is not only artificial but also shortsighted for the holistic educator. To fully approach an understanding of the world, an interdisciplinary approach is essential. The goal of Whole-Child educators is directly, consistently, and unabashedly focused on whole person development. One of the factors that determines the longevity of a culture is what it values. We saw in an earlier chapter that each civilization embraces a certain group of metaphors. These provide each culture with a unique worldview that frames how it solves problems (sciences), what it consider aesthetic (arts and humanities), and what is moral and ethical for its people (the good). Gardner refers to these Platonic ideals as virtues (Gardner, 2011).

Chapter Nine

Why Is the Learner-Centered Educator Interested in Positive Education?

A teacher plants the seeds of knowledge, sprinkles them with love, and patiently nurtures their growth to produce tomorrow's dream.—Anonymous

WHAT IS POSITIVE PSYCHOLOGY?

Martin Seligman (2002) introduced the "happiness formula" in his book *Authentic Happiness*. Seligman's insights and research studies eventually became the basis for what came to be referred to as positive psychology. This field emerged to counter psychology's penchant to focus on *mental illness* with a new emphasis on *mental wellness, happiness, and optimal functioning* (Gable & Haidt, 2005; Seligman & Csikszentmihalyi, 2000). Toward this end, researchers (e.g., Norrish & Vella-Brodrick, 2008; Linley et al., 2006; Gable & Haidt, 2005) have reported efforts to study the factors that foster human flourishing (thriving) to more fully understand the total human experience.

A response to Gardner's question posed in the last chapter—why should we care about *the truth, the beautiful, and the good*—is that by doing so, educators foster the development of what the Greeks referred to as a "eudaemon." Eudaimonia means flourishing and well-being. The eudaimon was the epitome of Greek education and, as such, prepared citizens for a life of flourishing. Ancient Greek mythology asserted that each individual possesses a "daimon" or spiritual companion that knows and guides the individual in finding his or her destiny in life.

In his book *Inching Towards Heaven's Door*, John Sieckhaus (2001) quotes the profound insight central to James Hillman's Acorn Theory: "Each life is formed by its unique image, an image that is the essence of that life and calls it to a destiny. As the force of fate, this image acts as a personal daimon, an accompanying guide who remembers your calling" (p. 140).

The above quotation suggests that a culture's education should provide its youth with the vision to realize their value, significance, and purpose, as well as the means and wherewithal to self-actualize. This notion, as simple as it seems, is nonetheless far removed from the philosophy of the American education system. Seligman (2011) concludes that human flourishing is the product of "happiness, flow, meaning, love, gratitude, accomplishment, growth, and better relationships" (p. 2). True happiness emerges from individuals experiencing meaning and fulfillment of their true nature (Ryan & Deci, 2001).

While eudaimonia sounds lofty and ideal, the factors that produce it contribute to living an authentic and meaningful life. Seligman (2002) reports that authentic happiness theory posits happiness is a function of five characteristics represented by the acronym PERMA. These characteristics include *positive emotion, engagement, relationships, meaning, and accomplishment* and, as such, produce a level of life satisfaction.

Positive emotion is the "cornerstone" of a well-being theory that is a function of happiness and life satisfaction. Engagement is what Csikszentmihalyi (2008) refers to as "flow." Flow experiences emerge when the individual is immersed in an activity that is inherently motivating and leads to experiencing optimal happiness and peak experience. When in flow, time appears to stand still and the individual may experience a *peak* or *optimal experience*. Meaning is finding one's purpose in life that provides fulfillment. While every individual has a purpose, discovering it is often a challenge and beyond our purview. To quote Mark Twain, "The two most important days of your life are the day you were born and the day you find out why."

POSITIVE EDUCATION

Adolescence is an emotionally turbulent stage in a child's development that impacts the psychosocial, academic, and vocational spheres of their lives (Sawyer et al., 2012). Lewinsohn et al. (1993) report that 20 percent of adolescents experience clinical depression by the end of their high school years. Moreover, according to Wickramaratne et al. (1989), depression is ten times higher now than fifty years ago. The explanation for this is most likely attributable to several non-school-related issues including increased divorce rates, stress, poverty, drug use, and violent crimes.

More recently, Mojtabai et al. (2016) report that the national trend in depression among adolescents has increased from 8.7 percent in 2005 to 11.3 percent in 2014. The upward trend seems to be continuing. In 2016, 12.8

percent of youths ages twelve through seventeen had a major depressive episode (MDE) during the past year and 9 percent experienced difficulty in completing schoolwork (Substance Abuse and Mental Health Services Administration [SAMHSA], 2017). Moreover, approximately 75 percent of mental illnesses occur within the first twenty-five years of life, which makes addressing adolescents and young adults all the more important (McGorry & van Os, 2013).

In a recent Australian survey of 18,994 young people ages fifteen to nineteen years (Cave et al., 2015), 38.4 percent reported being very concerned in developing ways to cope with stress, and school or study issues were the major concern for 33.6 percent of teens. Keyes (2009) found that less than 40 percent of young Americans were flourishing.

Thus, it is becoming essential for schools to include developing ways to foster well-being, along with academics. Toward this end, several countries have adopted a twenty-first-century whole-student curricular approach. This approach is focused toward social, emotional, moral, and intellectual development (Cain & Carnellor, 2008; McCombs, 2004; Palmer, 2003). Moreover, the number of educators being trained in positive education is on the rise (Green et al., 2012). In general, positive education seeks to apply the principles of positive psychology to promote student well-being (Green & Norrish, 2013; Oades et al., 2017).

Several researchers (Adler & Fagley, 2005; Emmons & McCullough, 2003; Polak & McCullough, 2006) report a positive correlation between gratitude and well-being. Otake et al. (2006) report individuals report higher levels of happiness with high levels of kindness. Kennette and Myatt (2018) report that teachers can nurture positive emotions in their classrooms by encouraging openness, respect, a sense of belonging, and applauding other students' successes.

An understanding of positive psychology is relevant to education as Howell (2009) reports flourishing adolescents reported higher academic achievement and performance than those experiencing only modest mental health. Therefore, support for educators who foster flourishing pays off in learner achievement. Several researchers (Chafouleas & Bray, 2004; Clonan et al., 2004) have noted an increased interest in applying the principles of positive psychology in schools. In chapter 2, we were introduced to ASCD's Whole-Child Approach initiative, as well as their Transformational Vision for Education in the United States. Both of these initiatives include integrating positive education and developing student well-being along with academic excellence.

Positive education has emerged as a practical and relevant application of positive psychology to classroom settings. Nonetheless, as Csikszentmihalyi (2008) asserts, before students can begin to reach for, much less achieve, their full potential, their minimal needs must be met (e.g., adequate food, sleep, shelter, and safety). This is especially relevant for children who come from impoverished households. Geelong Grammar School (GGS) located in Victoria, Australia, adopted Seligman's PERMA as well as health as the guiding principles on a whole-school basis to foster well-being (Vella-Brodrick, 2016).

GGS has integrated positive education into their school curricula for over a decade and, as such, is a fitting school for examining the effects of positive education. In a controlled study with GGS ninth-year students, Vella-Brodrick (2016) reported that positive education was responsible for decreased depression and anxiety as well as well-being (PERMA) of students. Moreover, students attributed that what they learned in the positive education program was a major factor in feeling more resilient, self-accepting, and confident in reaching their goals.

Furthermore, students reported using positive education learning strategies (e.g., expressing gratitude, resilient thinking, and effective problem solving) even outside of school events.

Diener and Seligman (2002) cite positive relationships, especially with their teachers (Guay & Senecal, 2016), as central to students developing a sense of well-being and therefore happiness. Therefore, it is essential that educators create a classroom climate that is conducive to fostering well-being by developing a good rapport with their students. Moreover, Baker et al. (2008) suggest that in order to promote a healthy classroom climate, educators need to get to know their students, show them they care, as well as demonstrate that they support their academic needs.

Social constructivists maintain that the learning process is a function of several factors including the relationships learners experience between classmates and their teachers. Berkowitz et al. (2017) have emphasized that character strengths and positive educational skill sets need to be integrated within the traditional academic curriculum in order to be effective. This is an important point that needs to be emphasized. Too many times when educators are asked to integrate a new strategy or teaching approach they do so in isolation of their curricular teaching and treat it merely as an "add-on."

Integrating positive educational practices means that the teacher is always mindful of opportunities during a lesson when they can capitalize on a "teachable moment." These teachable moments reinforce a student's character strength and/or use praise in a meaningful manner. This is especially the case for students who perceive they are less capable than their classmates.

Seligman (2011) emphasized the importance of "meaning" to an individual's sense of well-being. Therefore, educators need to design assignments that are relevant and personally meaningful to their students. Moreover, teaching, with the principles of positive psychology in mind, can benefit educators by making them more self-aware of their teaching. Educators aware of the significance of these principles to students' well-being are likely to approach them with empathy (Kennette & Myatt, 2018). Teaching from this perspective can provide educators with a greater sense of personal meaning and purpose.

Immordino-Yang's team at the University of Southern California concluded that brain growth during early to middle adolescence was "predictive of success in school, self actualization, relationship satisfaction and other positive indicators in early adulthood" (Immordino-Yang & Knecht, 2020, p. 1). This finding begs the question: *what do these growing nerve networks do and how can educators strengthen them?* Immordino-Yang and Knecht are researching these questions and in the meanwhile offer the notion that people create narratives about their world and their experiences in it.

Meaning-making narratives have neural correlates in the brain, and moreover, these neural networks predict how the individual will behave in the future (Immordino-Yang & Knecht, 2020, p. 1). Furthermore, the narratives teenagers told affected their dispositions of mind. These narratives reflected their inclination to be curious or compassionate, as well as use what they have learned to form values (Immordino-Yang & Knecht, 2020). Once again neuroscience supports the notion that what is essential for individuals, especially teens, is to find meaning in all they do in order to become effective learners.

For students, finding what they are learning in school to be meaningful and relevant to them is critical in becoming successful and compassionate people. *Educators who adopt a meaningful approach to learning and supporting the social, emotional, and cognitive development of their students will likely contribute to them creating meaningful narratives.*

Positive educational practices consist of developing approaches to augment students' strengths. These practices have been reported to:

1. aid educators in gaining a holistic perspective of their students (Bozic, 2013; Tedeschi & Kilmer, 2005);
2. engage and empower the learner (Bozic, 2013);
3. enhance the perceptions and expectations of their students (D'Amato, et al., 2005);
4. foster students developing a positive view of themselves (D'Amato et al., 2005); and
5. promote supportive and trusting student-teacher relationships (Bozic, 2013).

HOW CAN THE LEARNER-CENTERED EDUCATOR FOSTER COMPETENCY IN SOCIAL AND EMOTIONAL LEARNING (SEL) SKILLS?

How do educators foster the development of SEL skills? Fortunately, the brain continues to produce new brain cells every day, as well as create new neuronal connections between them. Therefore, from the perspective of education, the brain's neuroplasticity enables individuals to continuously learn new things throughout their lifetime. Over time new habits can replace old ones, and invalid concepts can be pruned back to make way for the emergence and consolidation of new ones.

Social and emotional learning (SEL) practices have been developed to foster students' emotional intelligence. Berman et al. (2018) assess that "how we teach is as instructive as what we teach. Just as the culture of the classroom must reflect social belonging and emotional safety, so can academic instruction embody and enhance these competencies and be enhanced by them" (p. 13).

Jones et al. (2017) divides SEL skills into three domains: *cognitive regulation* (attention control, inhibitory control, working memory/planning, and cognitive flexibility); *emotional processes* (including emotion knowledge/expression, emotion/behavior regulation, empathy/perspective/taking); and *social/interpersonal skills* (including understanding social cues, conflict resolution, and prosocial behavior) (p. 12). SEL skills are not developed in a vacuum but rather are integrated with the classroom and school setting at the level of peer-to-peer, student-teacher, and child-parent relationships.

Collectively, these practices offer a Whole-Child approach to learning and, as such, foster flourishing and academic achievement. Durlak et al. (2011) reported that meta-analysis studies conducted on K–12 students who were given social-emotional instruction scored 11 percent higher on achievement tests than students who didn't receive the instruction.

DEVELOPING COMPETENCY IN SOCIAL AND EMOTIONAL SKILLS

SEL researchers argue that educators have a responsibility to foster students' social and emotional skills. Toward this end, Jones et al. (2017) shared the recent research of SEL, as well as investigated twenty-five leading evidence-based SEL programs designed for elementary schools. Together they emphasize that children who can successfully manage their thoughts, attentiveness, and behaviors are more likely than not to have higher grades, as well as standardized test scores. Investigators (e.g., Durlak et al., 2011) affirm that current school-wide approaches to fostering SEL are making a meaningful difference in children's lives. To be effective, developing SEL skills must be integrated into the fabric of school and classroom instruction.

Jones et al. (2017) cite six factors as requisite for SEL programs to be effective:

1. *occur within supportive school and classroom contexts* (e.g., healthy classroom climate that promotes positive relationships);
2. *build adult competencies* with respect to SEL skills;
3. *acknowledge features of the broader community context* (building healthy family-school community partnerships);
4. *target a key set of skills* across multiple domains of development (e.g., emotional processes, social/personal skills, and cognitive regulation);
5. *set reasonable goals* (e.g., short- and long-term goals with respect to demonstrating competency in SEL skills); and
6. *incorporate SAFE* elements: (a) *Sequenced* activities that lead in a methodical way to developing SEL skill development; (b) students are provided with activities that require their *Active* participation in mastering skills; (c) students are provided with sufficient time to *Focus* on developing SEL skills; (d) teachers *Explicitly* define specific SEL skills to develop with their students. (pp. 21–22)

For a composite list of the twenty-five SEL leading programs, the reader can download Jones et al.'s (2017) report: *Navigating SEL from the Inside Out: Looking Inside and Across 25 Leading SEL Programs: A Practical Resource for Schools and OST Providers.*

SCHOOL-BASED BRIEF POSITIVE PSYCHOLOGICAL INTERVENTIONS (BPPIS)

Since Seligman and Csikszentmihalyi's (2000) seminal paper on positive psychology, a plethora of research studies and positive psychological interventions (PPIs) have been developed. These interventions were developed to promote well-being and individual character strengths. Fostering character strengths has become as important to educational leaders as teaching academic subjects. This new initiative has required rethinking the nature of professional development.

Today's educators need training in SEL skills, as well as how to integrate these into their classroom teaching. However, as with any new initiative, funding training workshops might only be realistic within certain school districts. Moreover, for the PPIs to be effective requires a commitment from teachers, guidance counselors, and administrators, as well as curriculum coordinators. Therefore, school-based brief positive psychological interventions (BPPIs) were developed.

What follows is a summary of a number of some BPPIs. There are several attractive features of BPPIs in that they can be implemented by individual teachers, integrated into the school curriculum, and used with students of any age and they do not require a lot of time to implement. Teaching SEL skills with BPPIs is a more feasible task than trying to develop these skills in a whole school forum.

Fredrickson's (1998, 2001) Broaden and Build Theory of Positive Emotions provides a useful model for understanding how PPIs affect well-being and achievement. Rathunde (2000) reports that Fredrickson's model has demonstrated how positive emotions enhance creativity and academic performance. Deci and Ryan's Self-Determination Theory (2002) suggests that when individuals experience autonomy, competence, and relatedness, they demonstrate increased levels of intrinsic motivation, engagement, and well-being.

What follows is a brief review of four PPIs: mindfulness, gratitude, positive relationships, and positive school climate.

Mindfulness

In 1979, Jon Kabat-Zinn developed, at the University of Massachusetts Medical Center, an eight-week program referred to as mindfulness-based stress reduction (MBSR) to treat a cadre of chronically ill patients who had not responded to traditional treatments. Since then, his MBSR program has not only been used widely but found effective in improving numerous physical and psychological illnesses including depression, chronic pain, eating disorders, and substance abuse (Grossman et al., 2004).

The benefits of mindfulness have been reported to last up to three years (Miller et al., 1995). Research studies have shown MBSR to be an effective PPI with children in school settings (Burke, 2010; Garrison Institute, 2005; Huppert & Johnson, 2010) to enhance attention and self-regulation (Goleman, 1995; Mayer & Salovey, 1997).

Several mindfulness programs have been developed and used throughout the United States. Mission Be (2020), which is an eight- to twelve-week program serves to:

- reduce stress,
- improve empathy,
- improve emotion regulation,
- improve emotional and physical well-being,
- increase focus,
- improve emotional intelligence,

- increase resilience, and
- improve school climate.

MindUp uses the latest in brain developmental research studies to maximize a child's learning and behavior. Likewise, *Learning to Breathe* (Broderick, 2013) and Amy Saltzman's *A Still Quiet Place* (2014) mindfulness approaches have been shown to reduce stress. Developing a mindfulness practice among school-aged children is relevant and has been shown to lead to greater levels of emotion regulation, empathy, and social skills (Baer, Smith, & Allen, 2004; Baer et al., 2006).

In school-based studies with kindergarteners, as well as middle school adolescents, emotion regulation has been found to be related to emotional well-being, social competencies, and academic achievement (Graziano et al., 2007). Thus mindfulness programs not only increase learners' sense of well-being; they positively impact their academic performance as well.

Gratitude

BPPIs have also been developed to foster gratitude. Emmons (2004) defines gratitude as "a sense of thankfulness and joy in response to receiving a gift whether the gift be a tangible benefit from a specific other or a moment of peaceful bliss evoked by natural beauty" (p. 554). Gratitude has been found to lead to an elevated sense of well-being (Adler & Fagley, 2005), life satisfaction, and optimism and decreased depression and envy (McCullough et al., 2002). Gratitude can be integrated into classroom teaching by creating a gratitude board whereby students can write what they are feeling grateful for that day on a sticky note and place it on the board whenever they enter or leave class. The nice thing about a gratitude board is that other students can also see what others are grateful for, especially if it is about them personally.

Positive Relationships

Positive relationships between peers, as well as with teachers, are essential to developing well-being in schools (Segrin &Taylor, 2007). Social support has been reported to ease stressful situations (Diener & Seligman, 2002) and increase happiness (Otake et al., 2006). Positive emotions have been reported to increase altruistic behaviors (Shankland, 2012), which in turn enhance one's meaning in life (Shek et al., 1994).

The tragic rash of school shootings over the past few years have typically occurred because the shooters felt socially excluded or isolated in some way from others. It is likely that none of these shooters had a wide number of meaningful relationships. Students who experience well-being, psychological health, and meaning in their lives are not prone to random acts of violence. These heinous acts spurred schools to develop advisory groups during the week whereby social and emotional skills could be taught in an integrated school context. Many educators use cooperative learning groups in their classroom teaching, which not only foster learning but also develop positive relationships and greater psychological health (Johnson & Johnson, 1987).

Positive School Climate

School and classroom climate need to be considered as factors that impact how students feel about themselves and others. Toward this end, several researchers report that a positive school climate is related to psychological well-being and academic engagement and performance. Additionally, a positive school climate enhances behavior (Berg & Aber, 2015; Durlak et al., 2011), student health, prevention of violence, and positive psychosocial adjustment (Cohen et al., 2009; Thapa et al., 2013).

Invitation Education is a whole-school approach designed to develop a positive school climate, which subsequently increases students' sense of well-being (Purkey & Novak, 2016). Invitation Education teaches a positive self-concept by serving to provide opportunities for people to perceive themselves as "able, valuable and responsible" (Purkey & Novak, 2016, p. 12). Recently, Reid and Smith (2018) set out to investigate student perceptions of school climate, as defined by Invitation Education theory, and students' subjective assessment of well-being. Their findings strongly support the notion that student perceptions of school climate are statistically significant and positively correlated to their perceptions of well-being.

Researchers from the University of Melbourne are vanguard leaders in studying the effects of integrating positive education into Australian schools. In a 2019 interview (as cited in Trudel, 2020), Dr. Lea Waters (2011), founding director of the Centre of Positive Psychology at the University of Melbourne, said this to describe the Visible Well-Being approach she developed: "a set of practices that teachers can flexibly bring into their own teaching practice so students directly experience well-being in the classroom, sports field, schoolyard, etc. This allows students to have the opportunity to build on their well-being in multiple classes throughout the day" (p. 4). Visible Well-Being relates the principles of positive psychology to visible thinking and visible learning.

SEARCH is an acronym of a framework that fosters development of six fundamental aspects of well-being including: strengths, emotional management, attention and awareness, relationships, coping and comprehension, and habits and goals (Trudel, 2020). Melbourne's Parkmore Elementary School began integrating positive education in 2012 and has since augmented their venture into positive education with growth mindset, mindfulness, visible well-being, as well as the SEARCH framework (Trudel, 2020).

Parkmore's initiative is a whole-school Whole-Child approach in that students receive positive education all day in every classroom and on the playing fields. Parkmore is certainly a standout exemplar of a whole-school approach to integrating positive education that other school systems would love to emulate. However, educators need to be able to assess the benefits of any new program before fully buying into it.

The state of Victoria, Australia, uses two surveys to assess the efficacy of their positive education initiative. The Student Attitudes to School survey evaluates student well-being as a function of effective teaching practice for cognitive engagement, social engagement, teacher-student relationships, learner characteristics and dispositions, school safety, and experience of bullying (Trudel, 2020). Turner and Pale (2019, as cited in Trudel, 2020) reported that scores on the Student Attitudes to School survey were significantly correlated with national standardized test scores.

The Behavior Intervention Monitoring Assessment System$_2$ is another useful instrument for schools to monitor the progress of a positive education initiative by tracking students' progress in the three areas of academics, social functioning, and behavioral concerns (Trudel, 2020).

The Benefit Mindset

Some researchers (e.g., Palmer, Zajonc, & Scribner, 2010) assert that educational systems are focusing too much on academic achievement at the expense of fostering students' emotional development. Ten years after Carol Dweck's book *Mindset: The New Psychology of Success* (2006) was published, educational researchers developed the Benefit Mindset that built upon Dweck's growth mindset to foster leadership and a deeper sense of meaning and purpose. The Benefit Mindset empowers students to be active participants in doing good deeds and creating well-being for themselves and society as a whole.

Today's world is facing a number of stressors issuing from political, social, economic, and environmental challenges to our well-being, safety, and health (Scharmer & Kaufer, 2013). The Benefit Mindset (Buchanan & Kern, 2017) "is a purpose-driven, leadership-based mindset that is redefining success: not only being the best in the world, but also being the best for the world" (p. 2).

The Benefit Mindset encourages individuals to do what they can to make a valuable contribution to society. Central to the Benefit Mindset is leading with purpose and doing what you can to encourage well-being for the collective good. There are several character strengths delineated by positive psychology that contribute to fostering the Benefit Mindset:

- perspective,

- love,
- kindness,
- social intelligence,
- social responsibility,
- teamwork,
- fairness,
- leadership,
- appreciation of beauty,
- gratitude,
- optimism, and
- spirituality.

SUMMARY

In addition to addressing the cognitive needs of students, the Whole-Child educator integrates social and emotional learning strategies into their classroom teaching. This chapter traced the origin of fostering social and emotional well-being to the emerging field of positive psychology. This branch of psychology arose as an alternative to only viewing the frailties, inadequacies, and dysfunctional behavior of individuals by traditional psychological therapists. Positive psychology focuses on fostering the well-being of individuals.

An outgrowth of positive psychology has been positive education. Positive education consists of social and emotional learning strategies that foster health and well-being of students. These social and learning strategies reduce students' anxiety and depression while enhancing their sense of well-being, character strengths, purpose, and meaning. Therefore, integrating SEL skills into classroom teaching has become an essential feature of education. Toward this end, several school-based brief positive psychological interventions (BPPIs) have been developed so educators can easily integrate them into their classroom teaching.

IV

Personal Demonstrations of Learning and Thinking

How Can the Whole-Child Educator Motivate Students to Take a Meaningful Approach to Learning?

Chapter Ten

The Whole-Child Educator Fosters a Growth Mindset

> *Learning is not attained by chance; it must be sought for with ardor and diligence.*—Abigail Adams

WHAT DOES IT TAKE TO MOTIVATE LEARNERS?

The Whole-Child framework offers a compelling model for educating students for the demands of living and working in the twenty-first century. Nonetheless, if students aren't motivated to adopt a meaningful approach to learning, then it matters little what curriculum is used. This begs the question: *why do some learners adopt a rote approach to learning, while others embrace a meaningful approach to learning?* Is it merely due to their cognitive ability? Or are there motivational factors that affect the extent to which a learner *wants* to or *believes* they can learn?

If motivational factors influence whether learners adopt and become proficient in using learning strategies, might the depth of understanding occur as a function of learners' level of motivation to use them? Can teachers foster students' proficiency in using learning skills? Learners develop competency in learning and thinking skills as a function of their motivational level and cognitive reasoning abilities. Therefore, it is safe to say that adopting and becoming proficient in the use of learning strategies must be a function of learners' level of motivation to learn. *Therefore, how can the learner-centered teacher motivate learners to become more adept at using learning and thinking skills?*

GROWTH VERSUS FIXED MINDSETS

Classroom teachers must create lessons that not only foster developing competency in using deep processing thinking skills but also demonstrate deep understanding. Encouraging students to adopt a growth mindset motivates them to not only learn but also develop the fortitude to remain engaged in academically challenging tasks. *This chapter will discuss how students can demonstrate a motivation to take a meaningful approach to learning.*

Dweck (1986) referred to students who primarily adopt *learning goals* as possessing a *growth mindset*. Growth mindset students perceive that ability can increase with effort. Students who possess a low affinity for *learning goals* possess a *fixed mindset*. Students with a fixed mindset perceive ability as a limited entity that cannot increase with more effort. Dweck's (1986, 1999), research demonstrated that praise is a double-edged sword depending on how it's used.

On the one hand, praising a student's *intelligence* fosters a fixed mindset, whereas praising a student's *effort* or process fosters a growth mindset. The reasoning here is that students who believe their intelligence is limited will perceive their ability is therefore limited, and that perception consequently confines them to adopt a fixed mindset (Dweck, 2006). Conversely, students who believe their intelligence can increase with effort and/or learning new skills perceive their ability can increase, thereby providing them with a growth mindset (Dweck, 2006).

Therefore, praising students on the basis of intelligence is potentially problematic for students who believe their intelligence is limited. Overall it is best to praise all students for their *effort* rather than *ability*, which some—those with a fixed mindset—believe cannot be increased.

One of the characteristics of students adopting a growth mindset is "grit," defined as tenacity, resilience, persistence, and perseverance in remaining engaged in a challenging task. A gritty person is not only conscientious and achievement-oriented but also is able to sustain their effort despite facing failure, setbacks, or difficulty. "The gritty individual approaches achievement as a marathon; his or her advantage is stamina" (Duckworth et al., 2007 p. 1088). As one can deduce, the growth mindset has a lot in common with grittiness.

Caine et al. (2011) explain the correlation between grit and the growth mindset on the basis of Gardner's multiple intelligences. According to Gardner, intelligence is not static but dynamic and based upon what the individual needs to do. Moreover, Caine et al. maintain that an individual's perception of intelligence can be retrained. *Educators need to keep in mind that learners' mindsets can change over time explicitly with teachers' emphasis on expending effort.*

Since intelligence is dynamic, a growth mindset can be nurtured. Keown and Bourke (2019) concluded consistent adult support resulted in third- and fourth-grade children remaining engaged after failure. Moreover, they demonstrated the drive to develop their intelligence—characteristics of a growth mindset.

Toward this end, Keown and Bourke cite the response of a fourth-grade special education student—Sally—regarding the support she receives from numerous adults: "My friends and my teachers, my principal and everybody. They encourage me by saying things that make me feel better. If I feel discouraged they tell me I can do it. They encourage me to continue to try harder and work harder" (p. 55).

Michael, another student in their study, supported Sally's response by saying, "I also feel encouraged at school and safe and very relaxing. My teachers and my classmates encourage me. The teachers at this school encourage me to do more things and tryout more and new things" (p. 56).

Other students in the study also stated that the positive support adults in their life, whether in school or their parents, often offered advice and support that fostered grit and a growth mindset. A recent report, commissioned by the Australian government, reviewed the Australian education system. The findings of the report stated: "Every young Australian should emerge from schooling as a creative, connected, and engaged learner with a growth mindset that can help to improve a student's educational achievement over time" (Department of Education and Training, 2018, p. x). There has been a proliferation of research studies validating Dweck's (1986) seminal work since she demonstrated that mindsets are beliefs that define an individual's intelligence as fixed or malleable. Moreover, there have been a number of published research studies exploring ways to foster a growth mindset. Toward this end, researchers have investigated strategies to develop students' responsibility for their learning (Dweck et al., 2014).

Children who are motivated by intrinsic factors are more likely than those motivated by extrinsic rewards to seek greater knowledge, experience more enjoyment in learning, and have a more positive self-image as learners (Pintrich & Schunk, 2002). Pintrich and Schunk concluded that intrinsically motivated learners, in contrast to their extrinsically motivated peers, are more persistent in remaining engaged in learning tasks. Therefore, it isn't surprising that Shernoff et al. (2003) report student engagement was highest when they experienced a balance between challenge and skill. They were most disengaged when they either lacked challenge or were presented with irrelevant assignments.

Therefore, it is essential that educators design lessons that maintain a balance between challenge and skill to keep their students actively engaged in the learning process. This is especially the case with respect to fixed mindset students who will likely withdraw from lessons that overly challenge their perceived ability. Overly challenging the fixed mindset student is likely to cause them to lose self-esteem and foster the belief that they are less competent than others.

The findings from Dweck's (Cain & Dweck, 1995; Heyman et al., 1992) research studies cite that mindsets can develop in children as young as three years old. Bialik and Fadel (2015) maintain that fostering the adoption of a growth mindset with children in the early grades is important. O'Connell et al. (2016) state that early on in a child's education represents a critical period for developing children's ability to become creative, entrepreneurial, resilient, and capable learners.

Dweck et al. (2014) established that in addition to working hard, noncognitive factors including mindset, social belonging, self-regulation, and self-control promote long-term learning and achievement. Boylan et al. (2018) also concluded that their survey results pointed toward several factors essential for success in learning: feeling safe, being competent in social and emotional skills, engagement, and motivation. These findings corroborate that noncognitive factors are requisite for successful learning (Dweck et al., 2014).

Therefore, it behooves teachers interested in aiding children in becoming lifelong learners to develop these noncognitive factors, as well as resilience, persistence, and perseverance characteristic of a growth mindset. Educators seeking to foster a growth mindset need to praise effort and persistence and abstain from giving feedback that emphasizes students' intelligence or ability. Doing so will encourage students seeking intrinsic rewards including learning for learning as an end itself rather than merely a means to an end.

Whole-Child educators are most likely to develop cognitive, along with noncognitive, factors in their students. Boylan et al. (2018) surveyed ninety-five Western Australian primary school teachers to investigate their perspectives on fostering a growth mindset. The consensus of the teachers surveyed was that while they understood the basis of the growth mindset, they lacked the strategies and methods to develop it with young children.

Recently, Dweck (2017) acknowledged the fact that teachers may not understand how to include teaching a growth mindset in their classroom teaching. This is not unexpected as it takes time for educational research findings to "filter down" to the classroom teachers in operational terms in order to integrate them into their classroom teaching.

Dweck (2009) cites questions raised by the American Association of School Librarians (AASL) with respect to their Standards for the 21st-century Learner (2007). The AASL standards delineate the "skills, dispositions, responsibilities, and self-assessment strategies that are necessary for a 21st-century learner" (p. 8). Furthermore, for each of these four requirements, they posed the following questions.

- For *skills*, they ask: "Does the student have the right proficiencies to explore a topic or subject further?"
- For *dispositions*, they ask: "Is the student disposed to higher-level thinking and actively engaged in critical thinking to gain and share knowledge?"
- For *responsibilities*, they ask: "Is the student aware that . . . 21st-century learning require[s] self-accountability that extends beyond skills and dispositions?"
- And for *self-assessment strategies*, they ask: "Can the student recognize strengths and weaknesses over time and become a stronger, more independent learner?" (p. 8)

Not surprisingly, Dweck's response to these questions is "no" for many American students.

Many classroom teachers are still employing an instructionist approach to teaching. This type of teaching fosters:

- development of surface instead of deep thinking skills,
- passive instead of active acquisition of knowledge,
- rote instead of meaningful approaches to learning, and
- a fixed rather than a growth mindset.

In light of this, it is little wonder why many American students are not being prepared to thrive in the twenty-first century.

The following are some tips on how teachers can promote the growth mindset:

- Teachers demonstrate they are growth mindset learners—*good role models*.
- Talk to students about fixed and growth mindsets and how they are subject to change if the learner chooses to think differently about intelligence and ability.
- It is essential that teachers *show* students *they believe* their intelligence is not fixed.
- Teachers need to help students to believe they *can improve*.
- Teachers need to ensure students know *how to improve*.
- Teachers offer problem/project-based learning in collaborative groups where pupils *take responsibility for their own learning*.

SUMMARY

What is argued here is that students' motivation to learn needs to be included as a causative factor in the development of deep understanding of a concept. As a result, the Whole-Child educator recognizes the role that learners' beliefs about themselves and the learning situation play in motivating them to engage and persist in learning tasks. Thus, it is plausible to suggest that the Whole-Child educator, who employs *constructivist strategies*, will foster students to adopt a growth mindset. Furthermore, these students should be able to demonstrate higher levels of understanding as a direct result of adopting learning goals. Therefore, adopting a growth mindset will foster a meaningful approach to learning.

V

Interpersonal Demonstrations of Learning and Thinking

How Do Learners Demonstrate Well-Being and Emotional Intelligence?

Chapter Eleven

How Do Students Demonstrate Competency in Interpersonal Skills?

Very little is needed to make a happy life; it is within yourself, in your way of thinking.—Marcus Aurelius

This book not only addresses the faulty assumptions of the current national educational policy but also champions a systemic change in how schools can develop and promote today's students to flourish as twenty-first-century adults. Chapter 1 discussed the major problems faced by Whole-Child educators teaching in an outdated American educational system. Chapter 2 contended that a systemic change was needed in the way schools are organized to foster learning and thinking in the global workspace. Chapter 3 explored the dimensions of the Whole-Child learner paradigm.

Chapter 4 petitioned the need of a new story for education. Chapter 5 compared and contrasted the teaching practices of the teacher-centered and learner-centered approaches. The latter is best implemented by adopting constructivist pedagogies for thinking and learning. Chapter 6 investigated the benefits of constructivist teaching in fostering a meaningful approach to learning. Chapter 7 discussed the skills needed to flourish in the twenty-first century. Chapter 8 lauded the benefits of an interdisciplinary curricular approach to the Whole-Child educator. Chapter 9 discussed why educators are interested in positive psychology. Chapter 10 extolled why constructivist educators can foster a growth mindset.

In summary, chapters 1–3 laid the rationale for recommending a systemic change in education that resulted in proposing the Whole-Child paradigm. In chapters 4–9, we examined the educator-based and district-based influences that affect learning and well-being. In chapter 10, we examined how students can personally demonstrate meaningful approaches to learning. In chapter

11, we will discuss the interpersonal demonstrations of learning situated in a social context. In so doing, we will have thoroughly discussed the four quadrants of the Whole-Child Learner Model introduced in chapter 3.

THE CODDLING OF AMERICAN STUDENTS

In *The Coddling of the American Mind*, Lukianoff and Haidt (2018) offer an intriguing and profoundly insightful explanation for the predicament of today's youth with respect to their emotional fragility. They explain this dilemma from the perspective that, unlike students of the past, when today's students react to real problems, they tend to display cognitive distortions that exaggerate and overstate the problem even to the point of feeling threatened by it.

Lukianoff and Haidt trace this newly emerged tendency to distort their way of thinking to "coddling" by well-intentioned but overprotective adults in their lives. They use the word "coddling" to mean an overemphasis on protecting children. However, unlike in years past, protection today is not merely with respect to protecting children physically but also emotionally. People, like systems, require stressors to learn, adapt, and grow. For instance, making mistakes or even failing is a common stressor. Yet when left to their devices, a child under the guidance of a caring teacher and/or parent learns how to turn mistakes into learning opportunities.

Taleb (2014) coined the neologism *antifragile* to mean the ability to transcend resilience and be able to withstand and bounce back from the trials and tribulations that come our way. This is similar to building up immunity to a disease. You fall ill but recover even stronger than before. Thus this is reminiscent of the quote attributed to Friedrich Nietzsche: "That which does not kill us makes us stronger." However, if the parent or teacher protects the child from making mistakes or failing, they will never learn how to convert them into learning opportunities. Somewhere along the line they will make a mistake or fail when neither parent nor teacher is around to "save" them, and consequently they will be unable to cope with the event.

In *The Black Swan*, Taleb (2010) asserted that in complex systems (including humans), unpredictable and unforeseeable events occur. He likens the predictable ones to white swans since most people always see them. Taleb uses the term "black swan" to refer to unexpected, and therefore unpredictable, events that occur in one's life. Some of the "black swans" are emotional rather than physical. Some cognitive behavioral therapists, in fact, expose their patients to the very stressors that cause them emotional distress in order for them to become desensitized to them.

Taleb also referred to coddled children as "fragile" in that they are so *rigid and "brittle"* that, like a China Doll, they "shatter" when a "black swan" comes their way. The irony is that to make children resilient and strong, you need to let them experience firsthand the "black swans" in their lives, thus increasing their *mental flexibility* to dealing with the unexpected, unfamiliar, or unwanted.

All of us are subject to "black swans" that occur without notice. You can't prepare for that which you don't know. This is similar to trying to coddle one's children. You cannot protect them from every unforeseeable and unpredictable event that will occur in their lives. Therefore parents need to be admonished—don't be too fastidious because overprotecting your children makes them more likely to be less resilient when an unlikely event occurs.

Lukianoff and Haidt (2018) cautioned:

> A culture that allows the concept of "safety" to creep up so far that it equates emotional discomfort with physical danger is a culture that encourages people to systematically protect one another from the very experiences embedded in daily life that they need in order to become strong and healthy. (p. 29)

Lukianoff and Haidt reported a noticeable discontinuity that San Diego State University psychologist Jean Twenge (as described in Twenge & Nolen-Hoeksema, 2002) observed in the emotional lives of students born after 1995. She refers to these kids as the iGen or the Internet generation. Interestingly, these kids have higher rates of depression and suicide than did the previous generation—the millennials. Moreover, this generation is overly obsessed with safety that is both physical and emotional in nature. Lukianoff and Haidt conclude that the iGen were the first to be raised by well-meaning but also overprotective parents and teachers.

Parents often confront educators with respect to their teaching methods when their child is not performing, as they "should." Students demand "do-overs" and make-up tests when they score below their perceived effort and ability. It is thus imperative that educators not only fight against fostering "fragility" but integrate strategies into their classroom teaching to foster "antifragility"—healthy and resilient children—who can become emotionally ready and successful when they enter an unpredictable world.

Therefore, children who appear emotionally deregulated and/or lacking in effective coping skills are likely the product of a coddled childhood. Self-regulation is a key characteristic of effective learners. This is a consequence of developing self-awareness and self-management and, as such, involves coordination between the *executive cognitive brain regions* and the *emotional brain* (Goleman, 2011). However, if the individual senses a real or imagined threat, the emotional system goes into overdrive and seizes control of the mind. When the mind is under duress, learning is compromised.

Thus, students who have poor emotion-regulation skills frequently fall prey to their emotional upheavals. These emotional outbursts negatively affect their learning and/or coping with the stressor. A likely candidate for this takeover would be the emotionally coddled child who hasn't developed the emotion-regulatory strategies for dealing with a stressful situation. Moreover, since these children tend to meet stressors with cognitive distortions, the situation is magnified. It is therefore important for children to develop healthy coping skills.

Examples of coping skills include mindfulness, physical exercise, meditation, yoga, as well as shifting one's focus or tapping (emotional freedom technique) among others. Children can develop emotion regulation by monitoring their thoughts and testing them against reality, as well as experiencing situations that may cause them a little emotional unrest. It is at that time that they apply coping skills. Moreover, it's okay to feel anger or be sad, scared, or even fearful *if* the situation demands those feelings. The problem occurs when a child imagines a threat or that they are in danger. The inborn stress management system between the brain and adrenal glands takes over, and the child is thrust into a "fight or flight" situation.

Students competent in Social & Emotional Learning (SEL) skills are less likely to fall prey to becoming "fragile." Research findings (Ladd et al., 1999; Raver, 2002) demonstrate that children competent in SEL skills:

- are more attentive,
- manage negative emotions,
- develop healthy relationships with peers and adults, and
- display task persistence.

Denham (2006) concluded that students competent in SEL skills:

- develop friendships,
- initiate positive relationships with teachers, and
- actively participate in classroom activities.

Moreover, SEL-competent students have higher grades and standardized test scores (Blair & Razza, 2007).

Durlak et al. (2011) defined a set of competencies used to assess SEL:

- recognize and manage emotions,
- set and achieve positive goals,
- appreciate the perspectives of others,
- establish and maintain positive relationships,
- make responsible decisions, and
- handle interpersonal situations constructively. (p. 406)

CHARACTER STRENGTHS

As discussed in chapter 9, Seligman (2011) asserts that well-being is a function of PERMA. Humans are social animals and have evolved two opposing types of behavioral responses to phenomena—*approach or avoidance* (Elliot & Church, 1997; Elliot & Harackiewicz, 1996; Harackiewicz et al., 1997; Harackiewicz et al., 1998). These emotional tendencies are a product of the pleasure and pain centers in the limbic system (emotional brain). Thus, humans seek to approach situations that will bring about pleasure and, conversely, avoid situations that will create pain and, as such, attempt to maximize PERMA.

Peterson and Seligman (2004) identified twenty-four strengths and virtues (e.g., kindness, social intelligence, humor, courage, integrity, etc.) that are fundamental to all five of these elements. *Therefore, students demonstrating these characteristics possess not only a state of well-being but also happiness.* Moreover, Peterson and Seligman organized these twenty-four character strengths into six categories: wisdom, courage, humanity, justice, temperance, and transcendence.

- *Wisdom* includes creativity, curiosity, love of learning, and perspective.
- *Courage* includes bravery, perseverance, honesty, and enthusiasm.
- *Humanity* consists of love, kindness, and social intelligence.
- *Justice* comprises social responsibility, teamwork, fairness, and leadership.
- *Temperance* is characterized by forgiveness, humility, prudence, and self-control.
- *Transcendence* includes appreciation of beauty, gratitude, optimism, humor, and spirituality.

Character strengths needs to be understood from the set of values held by individuals and their cultural milieu. Whole-Child educators can nurture and observe the following character strengths among their students: *a love of learning, perseverance, honesty, enthusiasm, kindness, social intelligence, teamwork, leadership, forgiveness, self-control, gratitude, optimism, and humor*, among others.

D'Amato et al. (2005) argue that character strengths should be developed systemically. Seligman et al. (2009) and Twenge and Nolen-Hoeksema (2002) cite positive psychological research studies whereby educators teaching skills relating to *well-being, positive emotions, resilience, engagement, and a sense of meaning* guide students to attain their full potential.

While positive education programs employ Seligman's PERMA framework, Norrish et al. (2013) suggest adding a sixth character strength—*positive health and resilience*, which like PERMA nurtures flourishing. *Educa-*

tors can identify students who demonstrate social and emotional well-being by observing a display of these character strengths.

Angela Lee Duckworth coined the word *grit* to represent learners' *resilience, ambition, and self-control*, as well as their *sustained persistence* to achieve long-term goals. These attributes are four of Seligman's twenty-four character strengths. Moreover, grit, along with perseverance, defines character strengths of growth mindset learners.

As we discussed in chapter 10, when growth mindset students are confronted with new academic challenges, they increase their effort and employ or learn appropriate thinking skills in order to solve them. Conversely, when fixed mindset learners are confronted with an academic challenge beyond what they perceive they are capable of resolving, they withdraw from the task. Moreover, the experience only goes to support their belief that they are incompetent learners.

Therefore, when challenged, growth mindset learners thrive while fixed mindset learners fulfill their *negative self-image* and view the experience as an indictment of their lack of ability. The consequence of this is their sense of well-being and happiness plummet along with poor interpersonal relationships. Therefore, students adopting a growth mindset demonstrate several of Seligman's twenty-four character traits including *perseverance, optimism, enthusiasm, self-control, and positive health and resilience*.

WHAT IS EMOTIONAL INTELLIGENCE?

In 1995 Daniel Goleman published *Emotional Intelligence*, which became a *New York Times* best-selling book. Goleman's book made emotional intelligence a pop culture description of a new type of intelligence. *Multiple Intelligences* author Howard Gardner subsequently referred to this intelligence as an example of his intra- and interpersonal skills. This newly identified intelligence was referred to as both EI, for emotional intelligence, or EQ, for emotional quotients in contrast to one's IQ or intelligence quotient.

EI described an individual's ability to manage their emotions, especially in social contexts. Therefore, EI has come to be coupled with social intelligence to signify one's potential to understand, empathize, and affect the emotional state of others. Goleman drew upon the research of Peter Salovey and John Mayer (1990). Mayer and Salovey (Mayer et al., 2004) define emotional intelligence (EI) as "the capacity to reason about emotions, and of emotions to enhance thinking. It includes the abilities to accurately perceive emotions, to access and generate emotions to assist thought, to understand emotions and emotional knowledge, and to reflectively regulate emotions so as to promote emotional and intellectual growth" (p. 197).

An individual's EI impacts not only their social and emotional states but also their ability to perform academic tasks. Bar-On (1996) developed the first scientific instrument to assess EI in relation to personal and professional success (Abraham, 1999). AbiSamra (2000) conducted a study investigating the relationship between EI and academic achievement. Their findings indicated that students with high grade point averages (GPAs) had higher EI scores when compared with those with lower GPAs. Bar-On and Parker (2000) conducted a correlational study and also found a significant relationship between EQ and GPAs.

Using Bar-On's emotional inventory, Sutarso (1999) analyzed the results of 138 college students. The results were subsequently analyzed with respect to three aspects of emotional intelligence: *compassion, self-awareness, and attunement*. Statistical analysis revealed a significant effect of gender on EI. Akbar et al.'s (2011) research study, with high school students, investigated the relationship between EI and academic achievement, gender, socio-economic status, level of parental education, urban versus rural region, and birth order. Descriptive statistics revealed a high correlation between all parameters with EI.

Marc Brackett is the founding director of the Yale Center for Emotional Intelligence. Brackett, as a protégé of Peter Salovey, defined EI as the ability to *perceive, use, understand and regulate emotions*. In a *Phi Delta Kappan* interview (Heller, 2017), Brackett described the center's major goal:

> The majority of our work focuses on school systems. The approach we've developed is called RULER. . . . But it's important to note that RULER isn't a program, exactly, or a one-size-fits-all intervention. . . . The heart of it is the training we provide to school administrators, teachers, staff, students, and families, helping them to understand and apply key lessons from the research. (p. 20)

The Yale Center for Emotional Intelligence has had much success with the implementation of RULER in many schools in Connecticut and across the nation. RULER is Brackett's anagram for five emotional skills whereby R stands for recognizing one's emotions, U for understanding those emotions, L for labeling those emotions, E for learning how to appropriately express those emotions, and R for being able to regulate those emotions.

The Yale Center for Emotional Intelligence takes an evidenced-based research approach to understanding and presenting their findings with respect to social and emotional learning (SEL) to area school systems. They base their definition of SEL on that recognized by the Collaborative for Academic, Social and Emotional Learning (CASEL). Brackett stated that his center approaches SEL differently than others in that "we put emotional skills development of adults at the core of building students' social and emotional capacities."

In the interview, Brackett disclosed that there are five roles the emotions play in education:

- how the emotions influence attention, memory, and learning;
- the role that emotions play in decision making, which is of particular concern to understanding the behavior and actions of adolescents who have yet to fully develop their executive control of emotions in light of their rational thinking abilities;
- the role of emotions in developing and maintaining social relationships, which is central to adolescents understanding themselves and how others feel;
- the role of emotions as the driver for mental health, which is germane to understanding the plight of adolescents whose fluctuating emotions are subject to "hair-trigger" events resulting in unexpected mood swings; and finally
- the role of emotions in creativity and performance.

Figure 11.1 illustrates the dynamic interplay between internal and external factors that affect the learning process. A learner-centered approach to teaching fosters the development and competency in deep process thinking skills, as well as a meaningful approach to learning. Taking a meaningful approach to learning results in constructing new concepts, as well as deconstructing and then reconstructing older ones to develop new understanding. Moreover, taking a meaningful approach to learning fosters adopting learning goals and, as such, a growth mindset.

A growth mindset fosters resiliency when confronted with new challenges. Therefore, a growth mindset drives the motivation of students to actively participate in the formation of their learning. Nonetheless, learning is not solely a cognitive process. It also requires the employment of noncognitive habits of mind and social and emotional influences that result in well-being. Moreover, the (1) quality of social relationships, (2) the teaching style, and (3) the classroom organization in which the learner is embedded affect how attentive and motivated students are.

Thus, the learning process is holistic and, as such, any change in either *internal* (perceptual, receptiveness, conceptual understanding, mindset, habits of learning) or *external* (classroom, social relationships, teaching style and practices, classroom organization) factors will have an impact on the learner in processing, assimilating, or accommodating the new concept into their knowledge base.

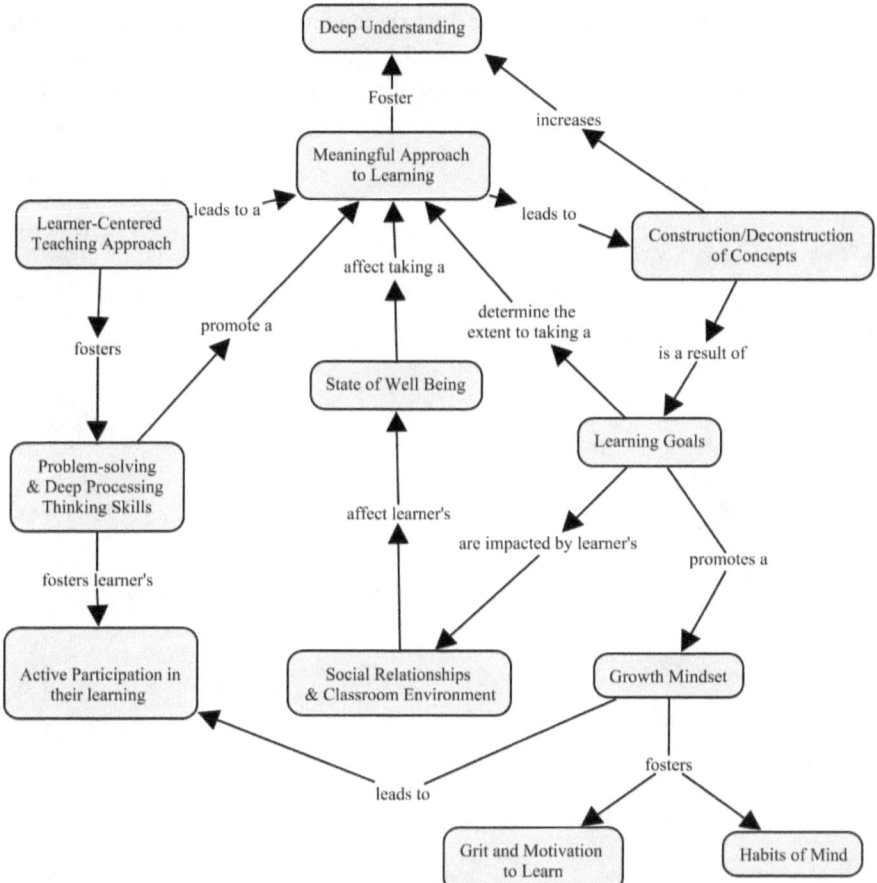

Figure 11.1. A Social-Constructivist Model for the Whole-Child Learner Perspective. *Author created*

SUMMARY

Students' social and emotional well-being directly impacts how and the extent to which they learn. Therefore, it is necessary for the Whole-Child educator to integrate social and emotional learning strategies into their classroom teaching. Whole-Child teaching fosters the development of the cognitive as well as social and emotional skills necessary to be a successful and well-adjusted individual. As we have discussed, we cannot view these as separate and unrelated skill sets. Rather, academic achievement is affected by learners' quality of relationships with their peers and teachers.

Additionally, if students are emotionally deregulated, they will be unable to concentrate, remain engaged, and perform well on learning tasks. In this book, we have looked at the four interdependent aspects of the learning process. The educator- and district-based influences provide the context for learning that is demonstrated both personally and interpersonally by learners.

Afterword

This book has taken the reader on a journey to understand the crucial importance of adopting a learner-centered approach fundamental to the interdependent aspects of the Whole-Child learner paradigm. This paradigm addresses children's academic, social, and emotional needs in order to succeed and prosper in the twenty-first century. Schools and classrooms need to become places where students can also grow and develop their creativity and imagination. If we are going to regain our status on the global stage as the vanguard educational system, America's educational leaders need to re-examine the shortcomings of their hubris and listen to the classroom teachers who have known all along what changes are needed.

With these criteria in mind, I set out to explicitly compare the stark differences between the twentieth-century teacher-centered and the twenty-first-century learner-centered approaches to teaching and learning. Toward this end, I argued that what was needed was nothing short of a *systemic change* in the ways students' academic, social, and emotional needs are met in order to thrive in the twenty-first century.

The premise of this book's argument was to examine not only the shortcomings of the twentieth-century teacher-centered approach to teaching but also to explain the fundamental educational advantages of adopting a Whole-Child approach to teaching. Each of the district-based and educator-based influences were discussed at length. These influences directly impact student learning. Therefore, both personal and interpersonal ways of demonstrating learning were discussed at length.

This dynamic model portrays each of the four quadrants as being *interdependent vertically, horizontally, and diagonally rather than serving as stand-alone aspects of the learning process*. This model mandates that the members of the entire school system must work interdependently toward integrating these learner needs. Hence, vital to this model is that the entire school system needs to not only accept but also adopt this philosophical change.

Consequently this systemic change will require a deep commitment by educators from all levels within the school system. Towards this end, a school system will need to offer a series of experiential Whole-Child learner workshops. These workshops will need to be attended by all pre-K to 12 staff and building administrators, as well as central office administrators and board of education members. The workshops will provide participants with the philosophy, teaching and learning strategies, as well as collaborative experiences requisite to foster social, emotional, as well as cognitive learning.

Additionally, a district-wide strategic plan committee will need to be organized. This committee must consist of representatives from the board of education; central office; building administration from pre-K, elementary, middle, and high school levels; as well as classroom teachers from each school level. The timeline for implementing the strategic plan will likely need to take place over at least four to five years in order to fully embrace a systemic change in transitioning from a twentieth- to twenty-first-century Whole-Child approach to teaching and learning.

Transitioning from the teacher-centered twentieth-century to the learner-centered twenty-first-century educational approach will, no doubt, require a commitment from the town governing body and taxpayers to financially support the changes and resources required to make the shift. Therefore, they will need to be apprised of this shift by publicly presenting the strategic plan to them so they can fully appreciate the reasoning underlying the request for additional financial support.

The most challenging aspect of adopting a district-wide Whole-Child approach will be overcoming the administrative hubris and inertia of adhering to the outdated teacher-centered, school-centric approach to teaching and learning. Nonetheless, participation in interactive Whole-Child workshops may provide a convincing rationale and motivation to embrace this twenty-first-century holistic approach to educating our youth.

In closing, the Whole-Child paradigm's educational framework provides educators at every level with an understanding of how to effectively foster learners' thinking skills, habits of mind, and mindsets to enhance their academic achievement. Moreover, this framework includes the vital social and emotional skills to initiate and maintain positive relationships with their peers, teachers, and parents.

References

AbiSamra, N. (2000). The relationship between emotional intelligence and academic achievement in eleventh graders. *Research in Education*, FED 661.
Abraham, R. (1999). Emotional intelligence in organizations: A conceptualization. *Genetic, Social and General Psychology Monographs, 125*(2), 209–224.
ACT. (2010). The condition of college and career readiness 2011. Retrieved from http://www.act.org/research/policymakers/cccr10/pdf/ConditionofCollegeandCareerReadiness2010.pdf.
———. (2011). The condition of college and career readiness 2011. Retrieved from http://www.act.org/research/policymakers/cccr11/pdf/ConditionofCollegeandCareerReadiness2011.pdf.
Adak, S. (2017). Effectiveness of constructivist approach on academic achievement in science at secondary level. *Educational Research and Reviews, 12*(22), 1074–1079.
Adler, M., & Fagley, N. (2005). Appreciation: Individual differences in finding value and meaning as a unique predictor of subjective well-being. *Journal of Personality, 73* (1), 79–114.
Akbar, M., Asghar, A. S., Khan, E. A., Akhter, M., & Riaz, M. N. (2011, December). Relationship between emotional intelligence and academic achievement among higher secondary school students. *Pakistan Journal of Psychology, 42*(2), 43–56.
American Association of School Librarians. (2007). Standards for the 21st-century Learner. Retrieved from http://www.ala.org/aasl/standards.
Amrein, A. L., & Berliner, D. C. (2003). The effects of high-stakes testing on student motivation and learning. *Educational Leadership, 60*(5), 32–38 and handbook.
Apple, M. W. (2006). *Educating the "right" way: Markets, standards, god, and inequality* (2nd ed.). New York: Routledge.
ASCD (2017). *The learning compact renewed: Whole child for the whole world*. Retrieved from http://files.ascd.org/pdfs/programs/WholeChildNetwork/2020-whole-child-network-learning-compact-renewed.pdf.
Baer, R. A., Smith, G. T., & Allen, K. B. (2004). Assessment of mindfulness by self-report: The Kentucky inventory of mindfulness skills. *Assessment, 11*(3), 191–206. doi: 10.1177/1073191104268029.
Baer, R. A., Smith, G. T., Hopkins, J., Krietemeyer, J., & Toney, L. (2006). Using self-report assessment methods to explore facets of mindfulness. *Assessment, 13*, 27–45. doi:10.1177/1073191105283504.
Baker, J., Grant, S., & Morlockl, L. (2008). The teacher student relationship as a developmental context for children with internalizing or externalizing behaviour problems. *School Psychology Quarterly, 23*(1), 3–15.

References

Baldwin, L., Flood, N., Naqvi, K., Ratsoy, G., & Templeman, E. (2017). *Green guide #15—Place-based education: An inter and multidisciplinary approach*. Windsor, Canada: Society for Teaching and Learning in Higher Education.

Banathy, B. H. (1991). *Systems design of education: A journey to create the future*. Englewood Cliffs, NJ: Educational Technology Publications.

Barnes, W. B., & Slate, J. R. (2011). College-readiness rates in Texas: A statewide, multiyear study of ethnic differences. *Education and Urban Society, 46*(1), 59–87. doi:10.1177/0013124511423775.

Bar-On, R. (1996). *The Emotional Quotient Inventory (EQ-i): A test of emotional intelligence*. Toronto, Canada: Multi-Health Systems, Inc.

Bar-On, R., & Parker, J. D. A. (Eds.). (2000). *The handbook of emotional intelligence: Theory, development, assessment, and application at home, school, and in the workplace*. San Francisco: Jossey-Bass.

Bell, S. (2010). Project-based learning for the 21st century: Skills for the future. *The Clearing House: A Journal of Educational Strategies, Issues and Ideas, 83*(2), 39–43.

Berg, J. K., & Aber, J. L. (2015). A multilevel view of predictors of children's perceptions of school interpersonal climate. *Journal of Educational Psychology, 107*, 1150–1170. doi:10.1037/edu0000027.

Berkowitz, M. W., Bier, M. C., & McCauley, B. (2017). Toward a science of character education: Frameworks for identifying and implementing effective practices. *Journal of Character Education, 13*(1), 33–51.

Berman, S., Chafee, S., & Sarmiento, J. (2018). *The practice base for how we learn: Supporting students' social, emotional, and academic development*. Consensus Statements of Practice from the Council of Distinguished Educators, Aspen Institute.

Bialik, M., & Fadel, C. (2015). *Meta-learning for the 21st century: What should students learn?* Center for Curriculum Redesign. Retrieved from http://curriculumredesign.org/wp-content/uploads/CCR-Meta-Learning-FINAL-Nov.-17-2015.pdf.

Blair, C., & Razza, R. P. (2007). Relating effortful control, executive function, and false belief understanding to emerging math and literacy ability in kindergarten. *Child Development, 78*(2), 647–663.

Boaler, J. (1999). Mathematics for the moment, or the millennium? *Education Week, 17*(29), 30–34.

Boyer, E. (1983). *High school: A report on secondary education in America*. New York: Harper & Row.

Boylan, F., Barblett, L., & Knaus, M. (2018). Early childhood teachers' perspectives of growth mindset: Developing agency in children. *Australasian Journal of Early Childhood, 43*(3), 16–24.

Bozic, N. (2013). Developing a strength-based approach to educational psychology practice: A multiple case study. *Educational and Child Psychology, 30*, 18–29.

Broderick, P. C. (2013). *Learning to Breathe: A mindfulness curriculum for adolescents*. Oakland, CA: New Harbinger.

Bronson, B., & Merryman, A. (2010, July). The creativity crisis. *Newsweek*. Retrieved from https://www.newsweek.com/creativity-crisis-74665.

Brown, P., Roedinger, H., & McDaniel, M. (2014). *Make it stick*. Cambridge, MA: Belknap Press.

Brownhill, R. J. (1981). Objectivity and subjectivity in Polanyi's personal knowledge. *Higher Education Quarterly, 35*(3), 360–372.

Bruner, J. (1990). *Acts of meaning*. Cambridge, MA: Harvard University Press.

Brusilovsky, P. (1999). Adaptive and intelligent technologies for web-based education. *Künstliche Intelligenz, 4*(Special Issue on Intelligent Systems and Teleteaching), 19–25.

Buchanan, A., & Kern, M. L. (2017). The benefit mindset: The psychology of contribution and everyday leadership. *International Journal of Wellbeing, 7*(1), 1–11. doi:10.5502/ijw.v7i1.538.

Burke, C. (2010). Mindfulness-based approaches with children and adolescents: A preliminary review of current research in an emergent field. *Journal of Child and Family Studies, 19*, 133–144.

Butkevicius, T. (2019). *How to build a brand story through storytelling*. Prestashop. Retrieved from https://www.prestashop.com/en/blog/brand-story-through-storytelling.

Cain, G., & Carnellor, Y. (2008). Roots of empathy: A research study on its impact on teachers in Western Australia. *Journal of Student Wellbeing, 2*, 52–73.

Cain, K. M., & Dweck, C. S. (1995). The relation between motivational patterns and achievement cognitions through the elementary school years. *Merrill-Palmer Quarterly, 41*(1), 25–52. Retrieved from https://www.jstor.org/stable/pdf/23087453.

Caine, R. N., Caine, G., McClintic, C. & Klimek, K. J. (2011). *Twelve brain/mind learning principles in action: Developing executive functions of the human brain*. Thousand Oaks, CA: Corwin Press.

Campbell, L., Campbell, B., & Dickensen, H. (2004). *Theory and development of multiple intelligences*. Boston: Allyn & Bacon.

Capra, F. (1996). *The web of life*. New York: Doubleday.

Cave, L., Fildes, J., Luckett, G., & Wearring, A. (2015). *Youth survey report 2015*. Mission Australia. Retrieved from https://www.missionaustralia.com.au/publications/research/young-people/doc_download/413-mission-australia-youth-survey-2015.

Center on the Developing Child. (2006). National Scientific Council on the Developing Child. Harvard University. https://developingchild.harvard.edu/science/national-scientific-council-on-the-developing-child/.

Chafouleas, S. M., & Bray, M. A. (2004). Introducing positive psychology: Finding a place within school psychology. *Psychology in the Schools, 41*, 1–5.

Chen, C. H., & Yang, Y. C. (2019). Revisiting the effects of project-based learning on students' academic achievement: A meta-analysis investigating moderators. *Educational Research Review, 26*, 71–81.

Christensen, C., Horn, M., & Johnson, C. (2016). *Disrupting class: How disruptive innovation will change the way the world learns* (expanded ed.). New York: McGraw-Hill.

Christou, T. (2016). Twenty-first-century learning, educational reform, and tradition: Conceptualizing professional development in a progressive age. *Teacher Learning and Professional Development, 1*(1), M.

Ciaccio, J. (2000). A teacher's chance for immortality. *The Education Digest*, 44–48.

Clonan, S. M., Chafouleas, S. M., McDougal, J. L., & Riley-Tillman, T. C. (2004, January). Positive psychology goes to school: Are we there yet? *Psychology in the Schools, 41*(1), 101–110. doi:10.1002/pits.10142.

Cohen, J., McCabe, L., Michelli, N. M., & Pickeral, T. (2009). School climate: Research, policy, teacher education and practice. *Teachers College Record, 111*(1), 180–213.

Connor, A., Karmokar, S., & Whittington, C. (2015). From STEM to STEAM: Strategies for enhancing engineering and technology education. *International Journal of Engineering Pedagogy, 5*(2), 37–47.

Costa, A., & Kallick, B. (Eds.). (2008). *Learning and leading with habits of mind: 16 essential characteristics for success*. Alexandria, VA: ASCD.

Csikszentmihalyi, M. (2008). *Flow: The psychology of optimal experience*. New York: HarperCollins.

Cuban, L. (2000, January). So much high-tech money invested, so little use and change in practice: How come? Paper prepared for the Council of Chief State School Officers' annual Technology Leadership Conference, Washington, DC.

———. (2001). *Oversold and underused: Reforming schools through technology, 1980–2000*. Cambridge MA: Harvard University Press.

D'Amato, R. C., Crepeau-Hobson, F., Huang, L. V., & Geil, M. (2005). Ecological neuropsychology: An alternative to the deficit model for conceptualizing and serving students with learning disabilities. *Neuropsychology Review, 15*, 97–103.

Darling-Hammond, L. (2007). Race, inequality, and educational accountability: The irony of "no child left behind." *Race, Ethnicity, and Education, 10*(3), 245–260.

———. (2010). *The flat world and education: America's commitment to equity will determine our future*. New York: Teachers College Press

References

Darling-Hammond, L., Barron, B., Pearson, P. D., Schoenfeld, A. H., Stage, E. K., Zimmerman, T. D., & Tilson, J. L. (2008). *Powerful learning: What we know about teaching for understanding.* San Francisco, CA: Jossey-Bass.

Deci, E. L., & Ryan, R. M. (2002). *Handbook of self-determination research.* Rochester, NY: University of Rochester Press.

Denham, S. A. (2006). Social-emotional competence as support for school readiness: What is it and how do we assess it? *Early Education and Development, 17*(Special Issue on Measurement of School Readiness), 57–89.

Department of Education and Training (DET). (2018). *Through growth to achievement: Report of the review to achieve educational excellence in Australian schools.* Retrieved from https://docs.education.gov.au/documents/through-growth-achievement-reportreview-achieve-educational-excellence-australian-0.

Dewey, J. (1897). My pedagogic creed. *School Journal, 54,* 77–80.

———. (1899). *The School and Society.* Chicago: University of Chicago.

———. (1900). Democracy in education. *Elementary School Teacher, 4*(4), 193–204.

———. (1916). *Democracy and education: An introduction to the philosophy of education.* New York: Macmillan.

Diener, E., & Seligman, M. E. (2002). Very happy people. *Psychological Science, 13*(1), 80–83. doi:10.3102/0034654313483907.

Duckworth, A. L., Peterson, C., Matthews, M. D., & Kelly, D. R. (2007). Grit: Perseverance and passion for long-term goals. *Personality Processes and Individual Differences, 92,* 1087–1101.

Durlak, J. A., Weissberg, R. P., Dymnicki, A. B., Taylor, R. D., & Schellinger, K. B. (2011). The impact of enhancing students' social and emotional learning: A meta-analysis of school-based universal interventions. *Child Development, 82,* 405–432.

Dweck, C. (1986). Motivational processes affecting learning. *American Psychologist, 41,* 1040–1048.

———. (1999). *Self-theories: Their role in motivation, personality, and development.* Philadelphia: Psychology Press.

———. (2006). *Mindset: The new psychology of success.* New York: Random House.

———. (2009). Who will the 21st century learners be? *Knowledge Quest, 38*(2), 8–9.

———. (2017). Growth mindset is on a firm foundation, but we're still building the house. Mindset Scholars Network. Retrieved from http://mindsetscholarsnetwork.org/growth-mindset-firmfoundation-still-building-house/.

Dweck, C., Walton, G. M., & Cohen, G. L. (2014). Academic tenacity: Mindsets and skills that promote long-term learning. Bill & Melinda Gates Foundation. Retrieved from https://ed.stanford.edu/sites/default/files/manual/dweckwalton-cohen-2014.pdf.

Education Reimagined. (2015). A transformational vision for education in the United States. *Educational Researcher, 32*(4), 3–12.

Eisner, E. (2002). *The arts and the creation of mind.* New Haven, CT: Yale University Press.

Elliot, A. J., & Church, M. (1997). A hierarchical model of approach and avoidance achievement motivation. *Journal of Personality and Social Psychology, 72,* 218–232.

Elliot, A. J., & Harackiewicz, J. M. (1996). Approach and avoidance achievement goals and intrinsic motivation: A mediational analysis. *Journal of Personality and Social Psychology, 70,* 461–475.

Emmons, R. A. (2004). Gratitude. In M. E. P. Seligman & C. Peterson (Eds.), *The VIA taxonomy of human strengths and virtues.* New York: Oxford University Press.

Emmons, R. A., & McCullough, M. E. (2003). Counting blessings versus burdens: An experimental investigation of gratitude and subjective well-being in daily life. *Journal of Personality and Social Psychology, 84,* 377–389.

Erickson, R. J. (1985). Play contributes to the full emotional development of the child. *Education, 105*(3), 261–263.

Fabriches, R. (2019). Spinoza, Emerson, and Pierce: Re-thinking the genealogy of pragmatism. Presidential address. *Transactions, 55*(2).

Fielding, M. (2001). Beyond the rhetoric of student voice: New departures or new constraints in the transformation of 21st century schooling? *FORUM, 43,* 100–112.

Fink, D. (2000). *Good schools/real schools: Why school reform doesn't last*. New York: Teachers College Press.
Fredrickson, B. L. (1998). What good are positive emotions? *Review of General Psychology 2*, 300–319.
———. (2001). The role of positive emotions in positive psychology: The broaden-and-build theory of positive emotions. *American Psychologist, 56*, 218–226.
Friedman, T., & Mandelbaum, M. (2011). *That used to be us: How America fell behind in the world it invented and how we can come back*. New York: Farrar, Straus and Giroux.
Gable, S. L., & Haidt, J. (2005). What (and why) is positive psychology? *Review of General Psychology, 9*, 103–110.
Gardner, H. (1993). *Multiple intelligences*. New York: Basic Books.
———. (2006). *Five minds for the future*. Cambridge, MA: Harvard Business School Press.
———. (2011). *Truth, beauty and goodness reframed: Educating for the virtues in the twenty-first century*. New York: Basic Books.
Garrison Institute. (2005). *Contemplation and education: A survey of programs using contemplative techniques in K–12 educational settings: A mapping report*. New York: Garrison Institute.
Geier, R., Blumenfeld, P. C., Marx, R. W., Krajcik, J. S., Soloway, E., & Clay-Chambers, J. (2008). Standardized test outcomes for students engaged in inquiry-based curricula in the context of urban reform. *Journal of Research in Science Teaching, 45*(8), 922–939.
Gergen, K. (1995). Social construction and the educational process. In L. Steffe & J. Gale (Eds.), *Constructivism in education* (pp. 17–39). Mahwah, NJ: Lawrence Erlbaum.
Ginsburg, K. (2007, January). The importance of play in promoting healthy child development and maintaining strong parent-child bonds. *Pediatrics, 119*(1), 182–191.
Gladwell, M. (2000). *The tipping point*. New York: Little, Brown.
Goleman, D. (1995). *Emotional intelligence: Why it can matter more than IQ*. New York: Bantam.
———. (2011). *The brain and emotional intelligence: New insights*. Florence, MA: More Than Sound.
Graziano, P. A., Reavis, R. D., Keane, S. P., & Calkins, S. D. (2007). The role of emotion regulation in children's early academic success. *Journal of School Psychology, 45*, 3–19. doi:10.1016/j.jsp.2006.09.002.
Green, L. S., & Norrish, J. M. (2013). Enhancing well-being in adolescents: Positive psychology and coaching psychology interventions in schools. In C. Proctor & P. A. Linley (Eds.), *Research, applications, and interventions for children and adolescents: A positive psychology perspective* (pp. 211–222). New York: Springer.
Green, L. S., Oades, L. G., & Robinson, P. L. (2012). Positive education programs: integrating coaching and positive psychology in schools. In C. van Nieuwerburgh (Ed.), *Coaching in education: Getting better results for students, educators, and parents*. London: Karnac.
Grossman, P., Niemann, L., Schmidt, S., & Walach, H. (2004). Mindfulness-based stress reduction and health-benefits: A meta-analysis. *Journal of Psychosomatic Research, 57*, 35–43.
Gruenewald, D. A. (2003, May). The best of both worlds: A critical pedagogy of place. *Educational Researcher, 32*(4), 3–12.
Guay, F., & Senecal, C. (2016). Students' school attachment and feelings of relatedness to teachers predict how they enjoy and value school learning activities. Presented at the Third Canadian Conference on Positive Psychology, Niagara Falls, ON.
Gultekin, M. 2005. The effect of project based learning on learning outcomes in the fifth grade social studies course in primary education. *Educational Sciences: Theory and Practice, 5*(2), 548–556.
Harackiewicz, J. M., Barron, K. E., Carter, S. M., Lehto, A. T., & Elliot, A. J. (1997). Predictors and consequences of achievement goals in the college classroom: Maintaining interest and making the grade. *Journal of Personality and Social Psychology, 73*, 1284–1295.
Harackiewicz, J. M., Barron, K. E., & Elliot, A. J. (1998). Rethinking achievement goals: When are they adaptive for college students and why? *Educational Psychologist, 33*, 1–21.

Hargreaves, A., & Fink, D. (2000). The three dimensions of reform. *Educational Leadership, 57*(7), 30–33.
Heller, R. (2017, May). On the science and teaching of emotional intelligence: An interview with Marc Brackett. *Phi Delta Kappan, 98*(6), 20–24.
Henrkisen, D., DeSchryver, M., Mishra, P., & Deep-Play Research Group. (2015). Rethinking technology and creativity in the twenty-first century transform and transcend: Synthesis as a trans-disciplinary approach to thinking and learning. *TechTrends, 59*(4), 5–9.
Heyman, G. D., Dweck, C. S., & Cain, K. M. (1992). Young children's vulnerability to self-blame and helplessness: Relationship to beliefs about goodness. *Child Development, 63*(2), 401–415. https://doi.org/10.1111/j.1467-8624.1992.tb01636.x.
Howell, A. (2009). Flourishing: Achievement-related correlates of students' well-being. *Journal of Positive Psychology, 4*(1), 1–13.
Huppert, F., & Johnson, D. (2010). A controlled trial of mindfulness training in schools: The importance of practice for an impact on well-being. *Journal of Positive Psychology, 5*, 264–274.
Immordino-Yang, H., & Knecht, D. (2020). Building meaning builds teen's brain. *Educational Leadership*. Retrieved from http://www.ascd.org/publications/educational-leadership/may20/vol77/num08/Building-Meaning-Builds-Teens'-Brains.aspx.
International Society for Technology in Education (ISTE). (2016). Standards for students. Retrieved from https://www.iste.org/standards/for-students.
Jackson, A., & Davis, G. A. (2000). *Turning Points 2000: Educating adolescents in the 21st century*. Williston, VT: Teachers College Press.
Johnson, D., & Johnson, R. (1987). *Learning together and alone*. Upper Saddle River, NJ: Prentice Hall.
Jones, S., Brush, K., Bailey, R., Brion-Meisels, G., McIntyre, J., Kahn, J., Nelson, B., & Stickle, L. (2017). *Navigating SEL from the inside out: Looking inside and across 25 leading SEL programs: A practical resource for schools and OST providers*. Cambridge, MA: Harvard Graduate School of Education.
Kennedy, M. (1992). The problem of improving teacher quality while balancing supply and demand. In D. Guildford and E. Boe (Eds.), *Teacher supply, demand, and quality* (pp. 65–108). Washington, DC: National Academy of Sciences.
Kennette, L. N., & Myatt, B. (2018). How the post-secondary classroom can benefit from positive psychology principles. *Psychology Teaching Review, 24*(1), 63–66.
Keown, S., & Bourke, B. (2019). A qualitative investigation of fixed versus growth mindsets of third and fourth grade students. *Education, 140*(2), 51–58.
Keyes, C. L. M. (2009). The nature and importance of positive mental health in America's adolescents. In R. Gilman, E. S. Huebner, & M. J. Furlong (Eds.), *Handbook of positive psychology in schools*. New York: Routledge.
Kinchin, I. M. (2001). If concept mapping is so helpful to learning biology, why aren't we all doing it? *International Journal of Science Education, 23*(12), 1257–1269.
Kohn, A. (2015). Progressive education: Why it's hard to beat, but also hard to find. Bank Street College of Education. Retrieved from https://educate.bankstreet.edu/Whole-Child/2.
Kuhn, T. (1962). *The structure of scientific revolutions*. Chicago: University of Chicago Press.
Ladd, G. W., Birch, S. H., & Buhs, E. S. (1999). Children's social and scholastic lives in kindergarten: Related spheres of influence? *Child Development, 70*(6), 1373–1400.
Lane-Zucker, L. (2005). Foreword. In D. Sobel, *Place-based education: Connecting classrooms and communities*. Great Barrington, MA: Orion Society
Lee, V. (2001). *Restructuring high schools for equity and excellence: What works*. New York: Teachers College Press.
Lewinsohn, P. M., Rohde, P., Seeley, J. R. & Fischer, S. A. (1993). Age-cohort changes in the lifetime occurrence of depression and other mental disorders. *Journal of Abnormal Psychology, 102*, 110–120.
Lichtenberg, J., Woock, C., & Wright, M. (2008). *Ready to innovate: Are educators and executives aligned on the creative readiness of the U.S. workforce?* New York: The Conference Board. Retrieved from https://www.amparents.org/wp-content/uploads/2013/10/ReadytoInnovateFull1.pdf.

Lindholm, J. A., Szelényi, K., Hurtado, S., & Korn, W. S. (2005). *The American college teacher: National norms for the 2004–2005 HERI faculty survey*. Los Angeles: Higher Education Research Institute, University of California, Los Angeles.

Linley, P. A., Joseph, S., Harrington, S., & Wood, A. M. (2006). Positive psychology: Past, present, and (possible) future. *Journal of Positive Psychology, 1*, 3–16.

Long, H. (2016, April 12). The new normal: 4 job changes by the time you're 32. *CNN Business*.

Lowenstein, E., & Smith, G. (2017, October). Making a world of difference by looking locally. *Educational Leadership*, 50–56.

Lukianoff, G., & Haidt, J. (2018). *The coddling of the American mind*. New York: Penguin Books.

Lusi, S. F. (1997). *The role of state departments of education in complex school reform*. New York: Teachers College Press.

MacDonald, G., & Hursh, D. (2006). *Twenty-first century schools: Knowledge, networks and economies*. Rotterdam, Netherlands: Sense Publishers.

Macy, J. (1991). *Mutual causality in Buddhism and general systems theory: The Dharma of natural systems*. Albany, NY: SUNY Press.

Maeda, J. (2013) STEM + art = STEAM. *The STEAM Journal, 1*(1), 34. doi:10.5642/steam.201301.34.

Marcon, R. (2002). Moving up the grades: Relationship between preschool model and later school success. *Early Childhood Research & Practice, 4*(1).

Martela, F., & Steger, M. F. (2016). The three meanings of meaning in life: Distinguishing coherence, purpose and significance. *Journal of Positive Psychology, 11*, 531–545. doi:10.1080/17439760.2015.1137623.

Mayer, J., Salovey, P., & Caruso, D. (2004). Emotional intelligence: Theory, findings, and implications. *Psychological Inquiry, 15*(1), 197–215.

Mayer, J. D., & Mitchell, D. C. (1998). Intelligence as a subsystem of personality: From Spearman's g to contemporary models of hot processing. In W. Tomic & J. Kingma (Eds.), *Advances in cognition and educational practice, Vol. 5: Conceptual issues in research on intelligence* (pp. 43–75). Greenwich, CT: JAI Press.

Mayer, J. D., & Salovey, P. (1997). What is emotional intelligence? In P. Salovey & D. J. Sluyter (Eds.), *Emotional development and emotional intelligence: Educational implications* (p. 334). Basic Books.

Mayer, R. (1996). Learners as information processors: Legacies and limitations of educational psychology's second metaphor. *Educational Psychologist, 31*(3/4), 151–161.

Mayer, R. E. (2002). Rote versus meaningful learning. *Theory Into Practice, 41*(4), 226–232.

McCombs, B. (2004). The learner-centered psychological principles: A framework for balancing academic achievement and social-emotional learning outcomes. In J. Zins, R. P. Weissberg, M. C. Wang, & H. J. Walberg (Eds.), *Building academic success on social and emotional learning: What does the research say?* (pp. 23–39). New York: Teachers College Press.

McCullough, M. E., Emmons, R. A., & Tsang, J. (2002). The grateful disposition: A conceptual and empirical topography. *Journal of Personality and Social Psychology, 82*, 112–127.

McGorry, P., & van Os, J. (2013). Redeeming diagnosis in psychiatry: Timing versus specificity. *The Lancet, 381*(9863), 343–345.

McQuillan, P. (1998). *Educational opportunity in an urban American high school: A cultural analysis*. Albany: State University of New York Press.

Miller, J., Fletcher, K., & Kabat-Zinn, J. (1995). Three-year follow-up and clinical implications of a mindfulness based stress reduction intervention in the treatment of anxiety disorders. *General Hospital Psychiatry, 17*, 192–200.

Mission Be. (2020). Mission Be's 8–32 week in-class mindfulness program. Retrieved from http://missionbe.org/mission-be-in-your-classroom/?gclid=CjwKCAjw4pT1BRBUEiwAm5QuR_Xh6QoDCGt7YtxmLP-i8DPetywuyKzABCxyRaL3p6Edv8XQN3NLEBoC-egQAvD_BwE.

Mojtabai, R., Olfson, M., & Han, B. (2016). National trends in the prevalence and treatment of depression in adolescents and youth adults. *Pediatrics, 138*(6), 1–10. doi:10.1542/peds.2016-1878.

Moran, M. (2006). Education is life: Technology, innovation, design and entrepreneurship for society. *Independent School*.

Muncey, D., & McQuillan P. (1996). *Reform and resistance in schools and classrooms: An ethnographic view of the Coalition of Essential Schools*. New Haven, CT: Yale University Press.

Narli, S. (2011). Is constructivist learning environment really effective on learning and long-term knowledge retention in mathematics? *Educational Research and Reviews, 6*(1), 36–49.

Nehring, J. H. (2006, February 1). Progressive vs. traditional: Reframing an old debate. *Education Week*, p. 32.

Next Generation Science Standards (NGSS). (2014). *Three dimensional learning*. Retrieved from https://www.nextgenscience.org/three-dimensions.

Noddings, N. (1995). A morally defensible mission for schools in the twenty first century. *Phi Delta Kappan, 76*, 365–368.

Norrish, J. M., & Vella-Brodrick, D. A. (2008). Is the study of happiness a worthy scientific pursuit? *Social Indicators Research, 87*, 393407.

Norrish, J. M., Williams, P., O'Connor, M., & Robinson, J. (2013). An applied framework for positive education. *International Journal of Wellbeing, 3*(2), 147–161.

Novak, J. (1998). *Learning, creating, and using knowledge: Concept maps as facilitative tools in schools and corporations*. Mahwah, NJ: Lawrence Erlbaum.

O'Connell, M., Fox, S., Hinz, B., & Cole, H. (2016). *Quality early education for all: Fostering creative, entrepreneurial, resilient and capable learners*. Mitchell Institute. Retrieved from https://www.mitchellinstitute.org.au/wp-content/uploads/2016/04/Quality-Early-Education-for-All-FINAL.pdf.

Oades, L. G., Steger, M. F., Fave, A. D., & Passmore, J. (2017). The psychology of positivity and strengths-based approaches at work. In L. G. Oades, M. F. Steger, A. D. Fave, & J. Passmore (Eds.), *The Wiley Blackwell handbook of the psychology of positivity and strengths-based approaches at work* (pp. 1–8). Oxford: John Wiley and Sons.

Obama, B. (2011) State of the Union Address. Retrieved from https://abcnews.go.com/Politics/State_of_the_Union/state-of-the-union-2011-full-transcript/story?id=12759395.

OECD Learning Framework 2030. (2018). *The future of education and skills: Education 2030*. Paris: Organisation for Economic Co-operation and Development.

Otake, K., Shimai, S., Tanaka-Matsumi, J., Otsui, K., & Fredrickson, B. L. (2006). Happy people become happier through kindness: A counting kindnesses intervention. *Journal of Happiness Studies, 7*, 361–375.

Palmer, P. (2003). Teaching with heart and soul: Reflections on spirituality in teacher education. *Journal of Teacher Education, 54*, 376–385.

Palmer, P. J., Zajonc, A., & Scribner, M. (2010). *The heart of higher education: A call to renewal*. New York: John Wiley and Sons.

Paramythis, A., & Loidl-Reisinger, S. (2004, February). Adaptive learning environments and e-learning standards. *Electronic Journal on e-Learning, 2*(1), 181–194.

Partnership for 21st Century Learning. (2019). *Framework for 21st Century Learning*. Retrieved from http://static.battelleforkids.org/documents/p21/P21_Framework_Brief.pdf.

Pearlman, B. (2006). Twenty-first century learning in schools: A case study of New Technology High School in Napa, California. *New Directions for Youth Development, 110*, 101–112.

Peterson, C., & Seligman, M. E. P. (2004). *Character strengths and virtues: A handbook and classification*. Oxford: Oxford University Press.

Pink, D. H. (2005). *A whole new mind: Why right-brainers will rule the future*. New York: Riverhead Books.

Pintrich, P., & Schunk, D. (2002). *Motivation in education: Theory, research, and applications* (2nd ed.). Upper Saddle River, NJ: Merrill Prentice Hall.

Pirsig, R. (1980). *Zen and the art of motorcycle maintenance*. New York: Bantam.

———. (1992). *Lila: An inquiry into morals*. New York: Bantam.

Polak, E. L., & McCullough, M. E. (2006). Is gratitude an alternative to materialism? *Journal of Happiness Studies, 7*, 343–360.

Purkey, W., & Novak, J. (2016). *Fundamentals of invitational education* (2nd ed.). Kennesaw, GA: International Alliance for Invitational Education.

Quigley, C. F., & Herro, D. (2016). "Finding joy in the unknown": Implementation of STEAM teaching practices in middle school science and math classrooms. *Journal of Science Educational Technology, 25*, 410–426.

Rathunde, K. (2000). Broadening and narrowing in the creative process: A commentary on Fredrickson's Broaden-and-Build Model. *Prevention & Treatment, 3*(6c), 1–6.

Raver, C. C. (2002). Emotions matter: Making the case for the role of young children's emotional development for early school readiness. *Social Policy Report, 16*(3), 3–19.

Ravitch, D. (2009, September 25). How to remake education. *NY Times Magazine*.

Reid, K., & Smith, K. (2018). Secondary students' self-perceptions of school climate and subjective well-being: Invitational education meets positive psychology. *Journal of Invitational Theory, 24*, 45–69.

Reid, R. (2019). Intercultural learning and place-based pedagogy: Is there a connection? *Learning at Intercultural Intersections, 157*. doi:10.1002/tl.20331.

Resnick, L. B. (1989). Introduction. In L. B. Resnick (Ed.), *Knowing, learning, and instruction*. Hillsdale, NJ: Lawrence Erlbaum Associates.

Ritchhart, R. (2015). *Creating cultures of thinking: The 8 forces we must master to truly transform our schools*. San Francisco: Jossey-Bass.

Ritt, M. (2016). The impact of high-stakes testing on the learning environment. Sophia, the St. Catherine University. Retrieved from https://sophia.stkate.edu/msw_papers/658.

Robinson, J., & Aronica, L. (2015). *Creative schools*. New York: Penguin.

Robinson, L., Smith, M., Segal, J., & Shubin, J. (2019). The benefits of play for adults. HelpGuide. Retrieved from https://www.helpguide.org/articles/mental-health/benefits-of-play-for-adults.htm.

Ruppert, S. S. (2006). *Critical evidence: How the arts benefit student achievement*. National Assembly of State Arts Agencies. Retrieved from https://files.eric.ed.gov/fulltext/ED529766.pdf.

Ryan, R. M., & Deci, E. L. (2001). On happiness and human potentials: A review of research on hedonic and eudaimonic well-being. *Annual Review of Psychology, 52*, 141–166.

Sahlberg, P. (2011). *Finnish lessons: What can the world learn from educational change in Finland?* New York: Teachers College Press.

Salovey, P,. & Mayer, J. D. (1990). Emotional intelligence. *Imagination, Cognition, and Personality, 9*, 185–211.

Saltzman, A. (2014). *A still quiet place: A mindfulness program for teaching children and adolescents to ease stress and difficult emotions*. Oakland: New Harbinger.

Sarason, S., & Seymour B. (1990). *The predictable failure of educational reform: Can we change course before it is too late?* San Francisco: Jossey-Bass.

Sawyer, K. (2019). *The creative classroom: Innovative teaching for 21st century learners*. New York: Teachers College Press.

Sawyer, S. M., Afifi, R. A., Bearinger, L. H., Blakemore, S.-J., Dick, B., Ezeh, A. C., et al. (2012). Adolescence: A foundation for future health. *The Lancet, 379*(9826), 1630–1640. doi:10.1016/S0140-6736(12)60072-5.

Saxe, J. G. (1872). The blind men and the elephant. In *The poems of John Godfrey Saxe*. Retrieved from https://en.wikisource.org/wiki/The_poems_of_John_Godfrey_Saxe/The_Blind_Men_and_the_Elephant.

Scharmer, C. O., & Kaufer, K. (2013). *Leading from the emerging future: From ego-system to eco-system economies*. San Francisco: Berrett-Koehler.

Seely Brown, J., Collins, A., & Duguid, P. (1989). Situated cognition and the culture of learning. *Educational Researcher, 18*(1), 32–42.

Segrin, C., & Taylor, M. (2007). Positive interpersonal relations mediate the association between social skills and psychological well-being. *Journal of Personality and Individual Differences, 43*, 637–646.

Seligman, M. (2002). *Authentic happiness*. New York: Atria.

References

———. (2011). *Flourish: A visionary new understanding of happiness*. New York: Free Press.
Seligman, M. E. P., & Csikszentmihalyi, M. (2000). Positive psychology: An introduction. *American Psychologist, 55*, 5–14.
Seligman, M. E. P., Ernst, R. M., Gillham, J., Reivich, K., & Linkins, M. (2009). Positive education: Positive psychology and classroom interventions. *Oxford Review of Education, 35*, 293–311.
Shankland, R. (2012). Bien-être subjectif et comportements altruistes: les individus heureux sont-ils plus généreux? *Cahiers Internationaux de Psychologie Sociale, 93*, 77–88.
Shek, D. T. L., Ma, H. K., & Cheung, P. C. (1994). Meaning in life and adolescent antisocial and prosocial behavior in a Chinese context. *Psychologia, 37*, 211–221.
Shernoff, D. J., Csikszentmihalyi, M., Schneider, B., & Steele Shernoff, E. (2003). Student engagement in high school classrooms from the perspective of flow theory. *School Psychology Quarterly, 18*, 158–176.
Sieckhaus, J. (2001). *Inching towards heaven's door*. Bloomington, IN: Xlibris.
Singapore Ministry of Education. (2005). Nurturing students. Retrieved from https://www.moe.gov.sg/education-system/nurturing-students.
———. (2015). Engaging our learners: Teach less, learn more. Retrieved from https://eresources.nlb.gov.sg/printheritage/detail/dbe9f1f3-efcb-4bce-917b-1040e95ea179.aspx.
Siyahhan, S., & Gee, E. (2018). *Families at play: Connecting and learning through video games*. Cambridge, MA: MIT Press.
Sizer, T. (1984). *Horace's compromise: The dilemma of the American high school*. Boston, MA: Houghton Mifflin.
———. (1992). *Horace's school: Redesigning the American high school*. Boston, MA: Houghton Mifflin.
———. (1996). *Horace's hope: What works for the American high school*. Boston, MA: Houghton Mifflin.
Smith, M. S., & O'Day, J. A. (1991). Systemic school reform. In S. H. Fuhrman & B. Malen (Eds.), *The politics of curriculum and testing: Politics of Education Association yearbook* (pp. 233–267). Bristol, PA: Falmer Press.
Sobel, D. (1999). *Beyond ecophobia: Reclaiming the heart in nature education*. Great Barrington, MA: The Orion Society.
———. (2004). *Place-based education: Connecting classroom and community*. Great Barrington, MA: The Orion Society.
Sparks. S. (2019, October). No progress seen in reading or math on nations report card. *Education Week*. https://www.edweek.org/leadership/no-progress-seen-in-reading-or-math-on-nations-report-card/2019/10.
Steger, M. (2012). Experiencing meaning in life: Optimal functioning at the nexus of spirituality, psychopathology, and well-being. In P. T. P. Wong (Ed.), *The human quest for meaning* (2nd ed.) (pp. 165–184). New York: Routledge.
Substance Abuse and Mental Health Services Administration (SAMHSA). (2017). Screening tools. Retrieved from http://www.integration.samhsa.gov/clinical-practice/screening-tools#drugs.
Supovitz, K. (2009, March). Can high stakes testing leverage educational improvement? Prospects from the last decade of testing and accountability reform. *Journal of Educational Change, 10*, 211–227.
Sutarso, P. (1999). Gender differences on the emotional intelligence inventory (EQI). *Dissertation Abstracts International, 125*(2), 209–224.
Symonds, W. C., Schwartz, R. B., & Ferguson, R. (2011). Pathways to prosperity: Meeting the challenge of preparing young Americans for the 21st century. Boston, MA: Pathways to Prosperity Project and Harvard Graduate School of Education. Retrieved from http://www.gse.harvard.edu/news_events/features/2011/Pathways_to_Prosperity_Feb2011.pdf.
Taleb, N. (2010). *The black swan: The impact of the highly improbable*. New York: Random House.
———. (2014). *Antifragile: Things that gain from disorder*. New York: Random House.
Tedeschi, R. G., & Kilmer, R. P. (2005). Assessing strengths, resilience, and growth to guide clinical interventions. *Professional Psychology: Research and Practice, 36*(3), 230–237.

Thapa, A., Cohen, J., Guffey, S., & Higgins-D'Alessandro, A. (2013). A review of school climate research. *Review of Educational Research, 83*, 357–385.

Thomas, D., & Seely Brown, J. (2011). *A new culture of learning: Cultivating the imagination of constant change*. Scotts Valley, CA: CreateSpace.

Trudel, S. (2020). Positive education down under: Melbourne schools create a culture of positive education. *International School Psychology, 48*(2).

Twenge, J. M., & Nolen-Hoeksema, S. (2002). Age, gender, race, socioeconomic status, and birth cohort differences on the children's depression inventory: A meta-analysis. *Journal of Abnormal Psychology, 111*(4), 578–588.

Vella-Brodrick, D. (2016). Optimizing the art and science of well-being in schools. *Communiqué, 45*(1).

Vygotsky, L. S. (1978). *Mind in society: The development of higher psychological processes*. Cambridge, MA: Harvard University Press.

Wagner, T. (2008). *The global achievement gap*. New York: Basic Books.

———. (2012). *Creating innovators: The making of young people who will change the world*. New York: Simon & Schuster.

Wagner, T., & Dintersmith, T. (2015). *Most likely to succeed*. New York: Scribner.

Walker, T. (2014). NEA survey: Nearly half of teachers consider leaving profession due to standardized testing. *News and Features from the National Education Association. NEA Today*. November 2nd.

Watson, A. D., & Watson, G. H. (2013). Transitioning STEM to STEAM: Reformation of engineering education. *The Journal for Quality and Participation*.

Wexler, A. (2018, November). What to do about standardized tests. *Forbes*. Retrieved from https://www.forbes.com/sites/nataliewexler/2018/11/15/what-to-do-about-standardized-tests/#2cd98c003074.

Wickramaratne, P. J., Weissman, M. M., Leaf, P. J., & Holford, T. R. (1989). Age, period and cohort effects on the risk of major depression: Results from five United States communities. *Journal of Clinical Epidemiology, 42*, 333–343.

Winterman, B., & Malacinski, G. M. (2015). Teaching evidence-based innovation (EBI) as a transdisciplinary professional skill in an undergraduate biology writing workshop. *International Journal of Arts and Sciences, 8*(2), 423–439.

Yates, L. (2007). Learning to "become somebody well": Challenges for educational policy. *The Australian Educational Researcher, 34*, 35–52.

Zernicke, K. (2015, March 24). Obama administration calls for limits on testing in schools. *New York Times*.

Zhao, Y. (2006). Are we fixing the wrong thing? *Educational Leadership, 63*(8), 28–31.

———. (2009a). *Catching up or leading the way: American education in the age of globalization*. Alexandria, VA: ASCD.

———. (2009b). Comments on Common Core Standards Initiative. *American Association of School Administrators Journal of Scholarship and Practice, 6*(3), 46–54.

Index

AASL. *See* American Association of School Librarians
AbiSamra, N., 123
abundance, 76, 80
accomplishment, PERMA, 96
Acorn Theory, 95–96
adaptive learning software, 26
adolescents, depression in, 96–97
affluence, 13, 76
African Americans, 8
Airbnb, 77
Akbar, M., 123
All I Really Need to Know I Learned in Kindergarten (Fulghum), xvi
American Association of School Librarians (AASL), 112
American Indians, 8
antifragile, 118, 119
Apple, 77
Aronica, L., 67
artificial barriers, tearing down, 46
arts: discipline for students, 90–91; interdisciplinary curriculum with learning and, 90–93; of teaching, 90
The Arts and the Creation of Mind (Eisner), 47
ASCD. *See* Association for Supervision and Curriculum Development
Asian Americans, 8
Association for Supervision and Curriculum Development (ASCD), 35, 36, 37
Australia, 97, 104–105
Authentic Happiness (Seligman, Martin), 95
autism, 78
automation, 76

Baker, J., 98
Bar-On, R., 123
beauty, with truth and goodness, 89
Behavior Intervention Monitoring Assessment System$_2$, 105
benefit mindset, 105–106
Berkowitz, M. W., 98
Berman, S., 100
Bialik, M., 112
The Black Swan (Taleb), 118
"The Blind Men and the Elephant" (Saxe), 31
Bloom's taxonomy, 54, 61, 64
Bourke, B., 111
Boylan, F., 112
BPPIs. *See* brief positive psychological interventions
Brackett, Marc, 123, 124
brain, 76–77, 78, 100
brief positive psychological interventions (BPPIs): benefit mindset, 105–106; gratitude, 103; mindfulness, 102–103; positive relationships, 103–104; positive school climate, 104–105;

school-based, 101–106
Broaden and Build Theory of Positive Emotions, 102
Bronson, B., 10
Buber, Martin, 47
Burt's Bees, 77

Caine, R., 110
The Cambridge Handbook of the Learning Sciences (Sawyer), 70
Capra, Fritjof, 33
CBL. *See* computer-based learning
CCSS. *See* Common Core State Standards
cells, brain neuroplasticity and, 100
character strengths, 121
China, 10
Christensen, C., 23–24, 25, 26
Christou, Ted, 15
classroom: stories, wanting to tell, 53–54; stories being told, 52–53; thinking and learning, orientations on, 51–52
climate change, 36, 81
clockwork paradigm, 1, 34
coddling, of American students, 117–118
The Coddling of the American Mind (Lukianoff and Haidt), 118
college readiness benchmarks, students and, 8
Common Core State Standards (CCSS), xvi, 12, 52
competency: computer-based learning (CBL), 24–26, 32; computer technology, 24; conceptual age; design and, 77; empathy and, 77, 78; high-order thinking skills and, 64; meaning and, 77, 80; play and, 77, 78–79; in SEL skills with learner-centered educators, 100; senses required for, 77–80, 86; social and emotional skills with, 100–101; story and, 77; students and issues with, 8; symphony and, 77, 78
constructivist approach: guided improvisation and, 70–71; high-order thinking skills and, 3, 68; to learning, 67–72; whole-child educators and, 67–70, 74, 87, 114
Costa, A., 84, 86
COVID-19, xii–xiii, 30

creating mind, 80, 81
creativity, 10, 71
"The Creativity Crisis" (Bronson and Merryman), 10
Critical Evidence (Ruppert), 90
critical thinking, 72, 87; ASCD report and, 36; dispositions and, 113; NTHS and, 85, 86; PBL and, 75; percentage of students without proficiency in, 8; skills, 32, 82; standardized tests and, 11; STEAM and, 92
Csikszentmihalyi, M., 97, 101
Cuban, Larry, 25
culture, 74; of learning and thinking, 13–14; transformation, 76
curriculum: arts and learning with interdisciplinary, 90–93; ASCD, 35, 36, 37; in Finnish schools, xii; learning and thinking with authentic, 47–48; narrowing, 11; one-size-fits-all, 12, 15

D'Amato, R. C., 121
Darling-Hammond, Linda, 35, 49, 75, 78
Deci, E. L., 102
decision making, 22, 124
Dell computers, 24
democracy, schools influencing, 10
Democracy and Education (Dewey), 49
Denham, S. A., 120
Department of Education, U.S., 22–23
depression, 96–97, 119
design, conceptual age and, 77
Dewey, John, 21, 27–28, 49, 86
Diener, E., 98
digital age, 2, 13–14
digital technology, 14, 74, 75
Dintersmith, T., 82
disciplinary thinking, 14
disciplined mind, 80, 81
dispositions, critical thinking and, 113
Disrupting Class (Christensen), 23–24
disruption: defined, 23; education with CBL as force of, 24–26, 32; education with PBE as force of, 27–32; education with PBL as force of, 26–27, 32; in systemic change, 23–24
Drawp for School, 30
Duckworth, Angela Lee, 122
Durlak, J. A., 120

Dweck, Carol, 105, 110, 111, 112, 113

education: CBL as disruptive force in, 24–26, 32; constructivism and whole-child, 67–70, 74, 114; Democracy and Education, 49; Department of Education, U.S., 22–23; in Finland, xi–xii, 10; *The Flat World and Education*, 49; *The Future of Education and Skills*, 49; *How to Remake Education*, 48; invitation, 104; as machine, 1; metaphors of twentieth-century, 51; NAEP, 8, 9; Obama on students and, 9; PBE as disruptive force, 27–32; PBL as disruptive force in, 26–27, 32; problems in, 7–8; progressive, 15, 16; "Progressive Education," 16; purpose of, 49; quality, 50; role of, 48–49; in Singapore, 10; systemic change and transformation, 22–23; systems as living processes, 21; *A Transformational Vision for Education in the United States*, 36; with whole-child framework, 46–47; whole-child paradigm and muddled, 34–35. *See also* positive education

education, transformation of: learner-centered educators and, 17; with learning and thinking, culture of, 13–14; problems with, 7–10; questions for, xii; with skills of students, 14–16; student underachievement and, 7–13; with testing, flaw of, 11–12

Education Reimagined, 36, 37, 84, 86

educators: twentieth-century practices, 62; whole-child, 74, 109–114. *See also* learner-centered educators

Einstein, Albert, 52, 53, 73

Eisner, Elliott, 47, 48, 54, 90–91

Emmons, R. A., 103

emotional intelligence: defined, 78, 121–122; reason and, 76; RULER, 123; Yale Center for Emotional Intelligence, 123

Emotional Intelligence (Goleman), 78, 122

emotions, positive, 96

empathy, conceptual age and, 77, 78

employers, skills most valued by, 10

engagement, PERMA, 96

entrepreneurship, 10, 83, 86
ethical mind, 80, 82
eudaimonia, 96
Every Student Succeeds Act (ESSA), xv, xvi, 12, 35, 52

Fadel, C., 112
Finland, xi–xii, 10
Finnish Lessons 2.0 (Sahlberg), xi
Five Minds for the Future (Gardner), 80
fixed mindsets, growth versus, 110–113
The Flat World and Education (Darling-Hammond), 49
Ford Motor Company, 77
Francis W. Parker School, 86
Fredrickson, B. L., 102
Friedman, Thomas, 14, 76
Fulghum, Robert, xvi
The Future of Education and Skills (OECD), 49

Gardner, Howard, xvi, 14, 25, 47, 54, 65, 89; arts and, 91; emotional intelligence and, 122; with minds, types of, 80–82, 86; STEAM and, 93; on thinking skills, 80
Gee, E., 79
Geelong Grammar School (GGS), 98
Gergen, K., 69
GGS. *See* Geelong Grammar School
Gladwell, Malcolm, 33–34
The Global Achievement Gap (Wagner), 82
global warming, 36, 81
Goleman, Daniel, 78, 122
Goodlife Fitness, 77
goodness, truth, beauty and, 89
Google Docs, 30
gratitude, BPPIs, 103
growth mindset: personal demonstrations of, 39; social and emotional skills and, xii; teachers and, 113; whole-child educators with fixed versus, 110–113
Gultekin, M., 27

Haidt, J., 118, 119
happiness formula, 95
Herro, D., 92

high-order thinking skills: competency and, 64; constructivist approach and, 3, 68; fostering, 83; learning and, 2, 47, 63, 74; model-building and, 69; NTHS and, 85; PBE and, 29; standardized tests and, 11
Hillman, James, 95–96
Hispanics, 8
Hong Kong, 10
Howell, A., 97
"How to Remake Education" (Ravitch), 48
human experience, 47, 95

iGen, 119
imagination, 67, 79
Immordino-Yang, H., 99
improvisation, constructivist approach and, 70–71
Inching Towards Heaven's Door (Sieckhaus), 95
Industrial Revolution, 1, 7
indwelling, 75
inertia, 23, 24, 128
Ingelhart, Ronald, 80
innovation, 10, 67
innovative thinking, 2, 9, 79
instructionist approach, to learning, 68
intelligence: praising students for, 110; students and emotional, 121–122
interdisciplinary curriculum: arts and learning, 90–93; truth, beauty and goodness with, 89
interdisciplinary thinking, 14
Internet generation, 119
intrinsic motivation, 16, 27, 69, 102
Invitation Education, 104

Japan, 9, 10
Jones, S., 100, 101
Jordan, Michael, 77

Kabat-Zinn, Jon, 102
Kallick, B., 84, 86
Kennedy, Mary, 8
Kennette, L. N., 97
Keown, S., 111
Keyes, C. L. M., 97
Kinchin, I. M., 74
Knecht, D., 99

Kohn, Alfie, 16
Kuhn, Thomas, 33

learner-centered educators: with competency in SEL skills, 100; role of, 17; social and emotional skills and, 1; as visionary systems thinkers, 65
learners: growth mindset and motivating, 109; redefining role of teachers and, 46; whole-child, 125, 128; whole-child paradigm and, xii, 37–41, 127. *See also* students
learning: *The Cambridge Handbook of the Learning Sciences*, 70; CBL, 24–26, 32; compact renewed, 35–37; constructivist approach to, 67–72; high-order thinking skills and, 2, 47, 63, 74; information-based, 8; instructionist approach to, 68; interdisciplinary curriculum with arts and, 90–93; interpersonal demonstrations of, 39; *A New Culture of Learning*, 74; Partnership for 21st Century Learning, 92–93; personalized, xvi, 13, 27, 32; principles of, 84; as process, 52, 62–65; as product, 51–52, 59–62; rote approach to, 60–61; teacher-centered versus whole-child, 73–74; thinking skills and, 74–75. *See also* thinking skills
Learning and Leading with Habits of Mind (Costa and Kallick), 84
learning and thinking: culture of, 13–14; student-centric approach to, 23, 24, 25, 27, 31, 37, 38
learning and thinking, new story of: classroom, 51–52; classrooms and telling, 52–53; classrooms and wanting to tell, 53–54; as curriculum, authentic, 47–48; education, role of, 48–49; education quality and, 50; metaphors of twentieth-century education, 51; as product or process, 45–46; as whole-child educational framework, 46–47
The Learning Compact Renewed (ASCD), 35, 37
Learning to Breathe, 103
left-brain thinking, 76–77
lessons, created by teachers, 61, 64
Lewinsohn, P. M., 96

Lila (Pirsig), 50
Lindholm, J. A., 8
living processes, educational systems as, 21
Long, Heather, 83
Lowenstein, E., 29
Lukianoff, G., 118, 119

machine, education as, 1
Maeda, J., 93
Makers Empire, 30
Mandelbaum, Michael, 76
Marcon, R., 87
Marcus Aurelius, 117
math levels, 8
Mayer, 69
Mayer, John, 122
MBSR. *See* mindfulness-based stress reduction
meaning, conceptual age and, 77, 80
meaning, PERMA, 96
Merryman, A., 10
mindfulness, BPPIs, 102–103
mindfulness-based stress reduction (MBSR), 102
Mind in Society (Vygotsky), 79
minds, types of, 80–82
Mindset (Dweck), 105
mindsets: benefit, 105–106; transcending current American, 46; whole-child educators with growth versus fixed, 110–113
MindUp, 103
Minecraft, 30
Mission Be, 102–103
model-building, high-order thinking skills and, 69
Mojtabai, R., 96
monolithic technology, 24
Most Likely to Succeed (Wagner and Dintersmith), 82
Multiple Intelligences (Gardner), 25, 122
Myatt, B., 97

National Assessment of Educational Progress (NAEP), 8, 9
National Scientific Council on the Developing Child, 34–35

Navigating SEL from the Inside Out (Jones), 101
NCLB. *See* No Child Left Behind
Nehring, J. H., 15
neuroplasticity, brain cells and, 100
Newsweek, 10
New Technology High School (NTHS), 85–86
A New Culture of Learning (Thomas and Seely Brown), 74
New York Times Magazine, 48
Next Generation Science Standards (NGSS), 21–22, 69–70
Nietzsche, Friedrich, 118
Nike, 77
No Child Left Behind (NCLB), xv, 12, 52
Nolen-Hoeksema, S., 121
nonconformity, 9
Norrish, J. M., 121
NTHS. *See* New Technology High School

Obama, Barack, xv, 9, 12, 13–14, 35
O'Connell, M., 112
O'Day, J. A., 22
Organisation for Economic Co-operation and Development (OECD), 49
Otake, K., 97
outsourcing, of white-collar jobs, 76

Pale, 105
paradigm, 1, 33–34. *See also* Whole-Child paradigm
Parker, J. D. A., 123
Parkmore Elementary School, 104–105
Partnership for 21st Century Learning, 92–93
PBE. *See* place-based education
PBL. *See* project-based learning
Pearlman, Bob, 85, 86
PERMA, 96, 98
personalized learning, xvi, 13, 27, 32
Peterson, C., 121
Phi Delta Kappan, 123
Pierce, Charles Sanders, 48–49
Pink, Daniel, 37, 47, 54, 91, 93; conceptual age senses, 77–80, 86; on cultural transformation, 76
Pintrich, P., 111
Pirsig, Robert, 50

PISA. *See* Program for International Student Assessment
place-based education (PBE), 27–32
play, conceptual age and, 77, 78–79
pollution, 36, 81, 82
Polyani, Michael, 75
positive education: BPPIs and, 101–106; defined, 96–99; with positive psychology, 95–96; SEL skills and, 100; with social and emotional skills, 100–101
positive emotion, 96, 102
positive psychological interventions (PPI), 101
positive psychology, 80, 95–96, 106
positive relationships, BPPIs, 103–104
positive school climate, BPPIs, 104–105
PPI. *See* positive psychological interventions
process: learning as, 52, 62–65; product and, 73
product: learning as, 51–52, 59–62; process and, 73
Program for International Student Assessment (PISA), 9, 68–69
progressive education, 15, 16
"Progressive Education" (Kohn), 16
progressive schools, 15
project-based learning (PBL): critical thinking and, 75; as disruptive force in education, 26–27, 32
psychology: BPPIs, 101–106; positive, 80, 95–96, 106

Quigley, C. F., 92

race, standardized tests and, 11
Race to the Top (RTTT), xv
Rathunde, K., 102
Ravitch, Diana, 48
reading levels, 8
reason, emotional intelligence and, 76
reform: defined, 15; efforts, 19–20; initiatives, criticism of, xvii; systemic, xv, 23. *See also* systemic change, transformation and
Reid, K., 104
Reid, R., 29–30
relationships, 96, 103–104

respectful mind, 80, 82
right-brain thinking, 76–77, 78
risk-taking, 61, 63
Ritchhart, Ron, 48, 54
Robinson, J., 67
Robinson, Ken, xvi, 14
Rogers, Laurette, 29
RTTT. *See* Race to the Top
RULER, 123
Ruppert, S. S., 90
Ryan, R. M., 102

Sahlberg, Pasi, xi–xii, 68
Salovey, Peter, 122, 123
Saltzman, Amy, 103
Sapir, Edward, 55
Sawyer, K., 70, 71, 78
Saxe, John Godfrey, 30–31
schools: AASL, 112; BPPIs and, 101–106; BPPIs and positive climate, 104–105; curriculum in Finnish, xii; democracy influenced by, 10; Francis W. Parker School, 86; GGS, 98; NTHS, 85–86, 86; Parkmore Elementary School, 104–105; progressive, 15; Student Attitudes to School survey, 105; transformation of, xi; twenty-first century exemplar, 85–86
school shootings, 103
The School and Society (Dewey), 49
Schunk, D., 111
science, 9, 21–22, 69–70
SEARCH, 104
Seely-Brown, John, 28, 74, 75, 79
SEL. *See* social and emotional learning skills
Self-Determination Theory, 102
Seligman, Martin, 95, 96, 98, 121
Seligman, M. E., 98
Seligman, M. E. P., 101, 121
SEMIS Coalition, 29
senses, conceptual age, 77–80, 86
Shark Tank (television show), 86
Shaw, George Bernard, 59
Shernoff, D., 111
SHTEAM, 93
Sieckhaus, John, 95
Singapore, 9, 10
Siyahhan, S., 79

skills: competency with social and emotional, 100–101; critical thinking, 32, 82; employers and valued, 10; *The Future of Education and Skills*, 49; SEL, 100; social and emotional, xii, 100–101; students and twenty-first century, 14–16. *See also* high-order thinking skills; thinking skills
Smith, G., 29
Smith, K., 104
Smith, M. S., 22
Sobel, David, 28–29, 47
social and emotional learning (SEL) skills, 100
social and emotional skills: competency and, 100–101; growth mindset and, xii; learner-centered educator and, 1
social-constructivist model, Whole-Child learner, 125
social justice, 16
social media, 13
South Korea, 9, 10
standardized tests, 11. *See also* testing
STEAM, 91, 92, 93
Sternberg, Betty J., xiii
A Still Quiet Place, 103
story, conceptual age and, 77. *See also* learning and thinking, new story of
STRAW program. *See* Students and Teachers Restoring a Watershed program
The Structure of Scientific Revolutions (Kuhn), 33
Student Attitudes to School survey, 105
student-centric approach, to learning and thinking, 23, 24, 25, 27, 31, 37, 38
students: with artistic discipline, 90–91; character strengths of, 118–120; coddling of American, 117–118; college readiness benchmarks and, 8; with competency issues, 8; emotional intelligence and, 121–122; ESSA, xv, xvi, 12, 52; intelligence and praising, 110; learners and, xii, 37–41, 46, 109, 127; Obama on education and, 9; PISA, 9, 68–69; with skills for twenty-first century, 14–16; underachievement, 7–13; whole-child paradigm and, xii, 37–41, 127

Students and Teachers Restoring a Watershed (STRAW) program, 29
suicide, 119
Sutarso, P., 123
Sweden, 82
symphony, conceptual age and, 77, 78
synthesizing mind, 80, 81
systemic change, transformation and: with CBL as disruptive force in education, 24–26, 32; with components aligned, 21–22; disruption in, 23–24; educational systems as living processes, 21; education and, 22–23; with PBE as disruptive force in education, 27–32; with PBL as disruptive force in education, 26–27, 32; systems, nature of, 19–20

Taleb, N., 118
teacher-centered learning, whole-child versus, 73–74
teachers: growth mindset and, 113; habits of creative, 71; lessons created by, 61, 64; with meaningful approach to learning, 63–64; with need to, 59–60, 62–63; with purpose demonstrated, 60, 63; redefining role of learners and, 46; risk-taking discouraged by, 61; risk-taking encouraged by, 63; role of, 53; with rote approach to learning, 60–61; science, 21–22; STRAW program, 29; whole-child, 2–3
teaching: art of, 90; whole-child, 15, 125
teaching practices: with learning as process, 62–65; with learning as product, 59–62
Teach Like Finland (Walker), xi
technology: adaptive learning software, 26; computer, 24; conceptual age and, 77; digital, 14, 74, 75; monolithic, 24; NTHS, 85–86
testing: with education, transformation of, 11–12; one-size-fits-all, xv; PISA, 68–69; standardized, 11
That Used to Be Us (Friedman and Mandelbaum), 76
thinking: disciplinary, 14; innovative, 2, 9, 79; interdisciplinary, 14; left-brain, 76–77; right-brain, 76–77, 78. *See also*

critical thinking; high-order thinking skills; learning and thinking
thinking skills: Gardner on, 80; learning and, 74–75; with schools, twenty-first century exemplar, 85–86; with teacher-centered versus whole-child learning, 73–74; for twenty-first century, 76–85
Thomas, Douglas, 74, 75, 79
thriving, in conceptual age, 78
TIDES, 86
TIMSS. *See* Trends in International Mathematics and Science Study
tipping point, 34
transformation, xi, 15, 76. *See also* education, transformation of; systemic change, transformation and
"A Transformational Vision for Education in the United States" (Education Reimagined), 36
Trends in International Mathematics and Science Study (TIMSS), 9
truth, beauty, goodness and, 89
Truth, Beauty and Goodness Reframed (Gardner), 89
Turner, 105
turning points, 20
Twain, Mark, 96
Twenge, J. M., 119, 121
twenty-first century: conceptual age and, 77–80; exemplar schools, 85–86; skills and students, 14–16; thinking skills for, 76–85

underachievement, of students, 7–13
United States (U.S.): Department of Education, 22–23; TIMSS and PISA rankings, 9; *A Transformational Vision for Education in the United States*, 36
University of Massachusetts Medical Center, 102
University of Melbourne, 104
U.S. *See* United States

Virtual ChemLab, 26
Visible Well-Being approach, 104
visionary systems thinkers, learner-centered educators as, 65
Vygotsky, Lev, 79

Wagner, T., 69, 76, 82, 86, 93
Wagner, Tony, xvi, 14, 26, 54, 82
Walker, Tim, xi
Waters, Lea, 104
We Are The Forest, 29
The Web of Life (Capra), 33
well-being theory, 96
white-collar jobs, outsourcing of, 76
A Whole New Mind (Pink), 76
Whole-Child educators: constructivist approach and, 67–70, 74, 87, 114; with growth versus fixed mindsets, 110–113; learner motivation and, 109
Whole-Child framework, 46–47, 128
Whole-Child learners, 125, 128
Whole-Child learning, teacher-centered versus, 73–74
Whole-Child paradigm: with education muddled, 34–35; framework, 128; interdependent facets of, 40; learners, xii, 37–41, 127; with learning compact renewed, 35–37; paradigm defined, 33–34
Whole Child Resolution, 35
Whole-Child teachers, 2–3
Whole-Child teaching, 15, 125
Whorf, Benjamin, 55
Wickramaratne, P. J., 96
The World Is Flat (Friedman), 14
writing levels, 8

Yale Center for Emotional Intelligence, 123

Zen and the Art of Motorcycle Maintenance (Pirsig), 50

About the Author

James Trifone holds a PhD in education from the University of Lancaster, UK. He is the academic director of the master of arts in learning and thinking (MALT) degree program, offered at the Graduate Institute in Bethany, Connecticut. This program consists of an innovative and learner-centered approach for pre-K to 12 educators who strive to develop and integrate a holistic twenty-first-century Whole-Child approach into their classroom teaching. He has authored numerous publications and conducted workshops at universities and national conferences on motivation in the United States and abroad. He is also the author of *From Being to Becoming: Living an Authentic and Meaningful Life*.

www.ingramcontent.com/pod-product-compliance
Lightning Source LLC
Chambersburg PA
CBHW020740230426
43665CB00009B/507